It Takes a
VILLAGE BOOKS

Chuck Robinson

Chuckanut Editions

Manufactured on the Espresso Book Machine
at Village Books in Bellingham, WA, USA

Edited by Sara Stamey

Book & Cover Design by Roderick C. Burton - Art & Design

Library of Congress Cataloging-in-Publications Data
Has Been Applied For.

ISBN 978-0-9842389-4-1

First Published By Chuckanut Editions, Bellingham, WA in 2010

For Dee,
my soulmate, best friend, and love of my life,
long before she became my business partner.

Contents

Foreword

Chuck and Dee Robinson love authors as only independent booksellers can. They talk up our books, honor our efforts, and, on occasion, meet us for a beer. They love their community, their industry, and, most importantly, each other.

They are passionate about what they do. "It would be impossible for a mom & pop store to survive if you looked at it as just a job," Chuck has said. "The business gets into your blood."

I first met Chuck and Dee in early 1995 at the Pacific Northwest Booksellers Association Show in Spokane, Washington. I was there to give a presentation on *The Nordstrom Way*, my first book with a New York publisher; PNBA was to be my first talk.

Neither my publisher nor PNBA was expecting big things from the book, so the room where I was to speak had just 25 chairs. Ten minutes before I was to begin, they were all filled. More and more people kept filing in. Organizers brought in 25 more chairs and then another 25. It was beginning to look like the stateroom scene from the Marx Brothers movie "A Night at the Opera." Ultimately, I was surrounded by 125 booksellers, some of them sitting on the floor, at my feet. Heady stuff.

After the presentation, the first person to come up to me was Chuck. After discovering we had a mutual friend who lived in Bellingham, we soon learned that we were the same age and had graduated college in the same year. A few minutes later, Chuck and Dee offered to put together an event for *The Nordstrom Way* in Bellingham. After the book was released a few months later, I spoke at a well-attended luncheon at the Northwood Hall, where we sold a ton of books. We've been friends ever since.

Over the years, as I've considered ideas for books, I've always called on Chuck for advice. He's an insightful sounding board and, on occasion, actually knows what he's talking about. (Sorry, Chuck. I couldn't resist.)

Around 2003, I began to piece together the elements of a book that eventually became *The Mom & Pop Store: How the Unsung Heroes of the American Economy are Surviving and Thriving*, which looks at the vital role that small, independent retailers play in helping to create and sustain our communities. I spent parts of the next several years traveling all over the U.S. to interview owners of restaurants, hardware stores, butcher shops, and the like.

Chuck and Dee were the very first mom & pop store owners I interviewed for the book. Sitting in the Colophon Cafe on the lower level of the old store, they shared the story of their journey from the Midwest to the Pacific Northwest, where they reinvented themselves as booksellers in 1980. Theirs is a quintessential American story of restiveness, soul-searching, self-discovery, and finally, connection—to their neighborhood, their community, their industry, and the rest of the world, all from a bookstore in little Bellingham, Washington.

"What has thrilled us the most is creating the kind of store we wanted and having the community embrace it," Dee told me. "Now, it has a life of its own." When local companies are trying to lure prospective employees to relocate, they bring them to the store. "People tell us that one of their main determinants in moving to Bellingham is Village Books."

It's impossible to imagine what Fairhaven would be like without Village Books; kind of like Bedford Falls devoid of Bailey Building & Loan. Chuck, Dee and their staff involve themselves in virtually every aspect of life and every worthy cause in Bellingham and Whatcom County. The Robinsons fight for the First Amendment and for the free exchange of ideas, including ideas with which they disagree.

"We're not in the business of selling books," Chuck says. "The grocery store and the drugstore are in the business of selling books. We would like to sell the books on our shelves. But our business is your coming into the store looking for a certain book or idea and our ability to connect you with that book or idea."

Surviving 30 years as an independent retailer—particularly a bookseller—is an heroic feat. One of the reasons that the Robinsons have endured is that they have always understood that they are running a business; not a hobby. If the business doesn't work, then all the noble efforts in the world will go for naught. "If you're opening a bookstore because you love reading books," Chuck tells aspiring booksellers, "then become a night watchman, because you'll be able to read more books that way."

Many independent stores begin to wind down when the owners stop moving forward. One of the recurring themes in *It Takes a Village Books* is adapting to change and keeping pace with the times. Proof of that is the book you are holding in your hand, which is published by Chuck and Dee's own imprint, Chuckanut Editions, and printed on the store's Espresso Book Machine. You can't get more mom & pop than that.

You, dear reader, are in for treat. Chuck is adroit at spinning wonderful personal yarns—about employees, customers, community leaders, literary notables (from Eudora Welty to Stephen King, Tom Robbins to Maya Angelou), four U.S. presidents, Margaret Thatcher, and the eruption of Mt. St. Helens. Not bad for a couple of kids from Illinois.

So, congratulations, Chuck and Dee. Speaking on behalf of every author who has ever given a reading at Village Books or who has met you along the way, thank you for your passion and persistence, your love of ideas, your sense of community, and your ability to make us all feel welcome. How about another 30 years?

– Robert Spector, Seattle

Introduction

I'm often asked if I'm a writer. Perhaps it's the connection with the literary profession that suggests I should be, but with each such inquiry I've asserted that I am not. Now I've proven it.

This is not an attempt at a literary masterpiece. It is simply the rambling story of Village Books over the past thirty years, as I remember it. I've tried to respond to many of the questions we've been asked in a bit more depth than the quips I've sometimes offered—Q: How did you get to Bellingham? A: I-90; Q: What prompted you to begin a bookstore? A: A moment of insanity.

The journey of putting this book together has been both exciting and exasperating. I've reread all of the newsletters and *Chuckanut Readers* we've published. I've rifled through files of clippings and correspondence. I've sorted through hundreds of photographs. I've plumbed the depths of my memory, Dee's memory, and the gray cells of many friends and colleagues. Most of that was great fun, and it helped me put nearly half of my life into perspective.

Deciding what to include and what to leave out has been challenging. I'm certain there are readers who won't care about some of the things I've recorded here. Others might want to know more about the events I mention. I've often been asked about the authors, politicians, and celebrities we've met. Some will enjoy the accounts of those encounters, while others will likely tire of the name-dropping.

The book is also a bit of a love story. It's about caring for a community in much the same way we care for those we're closest to. Not the starry-eyed, heart-a-twitter kind of love we "fall" in, but the deep, abiding love we "grow" into when we know someone well, when we really get involved with them. This is about becoming involved with a community and falling deeply in love with it.

Without the encouragement and early coaching of Bliss Goldstein, there would be no book, and without the patient and thoughtful editing of Sara Stamey, the book would be unreadable.

For the journey itself I am deeply indebted to many. Each person who has worked at Village Books and Paper Dreams has left his or her mark in some way. A number of those folks are mentioned in the book, but I am equally grateful to those who are not. The list, after thirty years, has grown far too long to itemize here.

The same is true for my many friends and colleagues in bookselling. Without their guidance and advice, the journey would have ended long ago. I'll also resist naming them here, but my friends, you do know who you are.

I hope you enjoy the book. If you truly want to know more, look for Volume Two... in another thirty years.

Chapter 1

The Journey Begins
1978–1980

"Hey! Let's open a bookstore."

Dee just stared at me, then laughed. "Yes! It's perfect—we both love books."

We were both small-town Midwesterners setting out on a cross-country trip to find our passion—just like Judy Garland and Mickey Rooney when they decided to "put on a show." The year was 1979.

Our own particular vaudeville production would immerse us in travels to study bookstores and West Coast communities and learn a business we knew nothing about as special-education teachers on leaves of absence. But within a year we would be sitting on the floor of an historic building in not-yet-bustling Fairhaven, thinking about all the advice against starting a business in a recession, staring at the empty bookshelves we had built by hand, and waiting for our first book order that was late in arriving for opening day.

"Do you think I should have kept my mouth shut, back in Illinois?" Dee asked.

"Sometimes I think I'd just like to be rid of all of this and take off to travel." Dee was looking out the window of our home near East Moline, Illinois. It was late fall of 1978.

I couldn't believe Dee had said that. Generally the more

impulsive, I might have suggested we take off right then, but saner thoughts prevailed and we began a conversation that led us step-by-step through divesting ourselves of most of our possessions, buying and remodeling an older motorhome, selling our house and hitting the road for—we thought—a one-year, round-the-country trip.

Dee and I had been married for nearly eleven years. I'd love to say that I swept her off her feet the first time we met, but the only reason she might have fallen that night was that she was on roller skates. It was Freshmen orientation week at Sioux Falls College—now the University of Sioux Falls—and though I tried to impress her, I failed.

We ended up hanging out in the same group, but it took some time to get her to go out with me. We dated off and on during the late fall and early winter of that school year and then drifted apart when she began dating an older student and I took up with a townie. But spring arrived with Cupid's arrow, and we began seeing each other again, then "going steady." On Dee's birthday that October, we were engaged, and during Christmas break of our Junior year, we were married in the midst of a blizzard in Dee's hometown of Hastings, Nebraska.

I was born and raised in a small town in the middle of corn country. That Illinois hamlet was an ideal place for a kid in the '50s and '60s. I grew up playing baseball and football, riding my bike, delivering newspapers, swimming in the local lake in the summer, and ice skating and sledding in the winter. I was a Cub Scout and, briefly, a Boy Scout. Later, when I read Bill Bryson's book, *The Life and Times of the Thunderbolt Kid*, I realized he had described my growing up years. Bryson is just four years younger and spent his childhood about two hundred miles to the west of my hometown. He describes two huge differences between those years and now.

The first is that there were lots of kids around. Bryson says, "America had thirty-two million children aged twelve or under in the mid-1950s... So there were kids everywhere, all the time, in densities now unimaginable, but especially whenever anything interesting or unusual happened." He goes on to say, "The other difference from those days was that kids were always outdoors—I knew kids who were pushed out the door at eight in the morning and not allowed back in until five unless they were on fire or actively bleeding—and they were always looking for something to do."

Bryson summed it up: "Life in Kid World, wherever you went, was unsupervised, unregulated, and robustly—at times insanely—physical, and yet it was a remarkably peaceful place." That was the world I knew as a child.

Dee was born in the small Iowa town of Manchester but moved to Hastings, Nebraska, when she was fifteen months old. Though Hastings was several times the size of my hometown, it was not a bustling metropolis, so Dee's childhood was not unlike my own bucolic Midwestern upbringing. She was a Brownie and a Girl Scout, participated in 4-H, attended church camp, and on many summer afternoons rode her bike to the city swimming pool. Bryson's childhood also resonates with her.

By 1978, ten years of working in education had brought us to this Sunday afternoon in the living room of a house we'd built and filled, just three years earlier. Life was good, but we were both a bit restless.

It's an amazing testimony to the power of words. Dee's one sentence—twenty syllables—would change our lives.

But it was only November. We were less than three months into a school year, and there was a lot of planning and work to be done before we could leave.

The nine months between that first conversation and the day

we hit the road in our motorhome were an intense values-clari-fication exercise. It was our first time to shed many possessions. That's never easy, but a few garage sales and an elaborate silent auction got us down to what we could carry in the motorhome and a small vanload of stored items.

In *Clear Your Clutter With Feng Shui*, Karen Kingston describes her method of deciding whether or not to keep an item. She recommends that you pick up the object and ask your-self, "Does this bring me joy?" When I read her book, many years after our purging experience, I realized that was exactly what we had done, and at that point in our lives, I doubt either of us had ever heard of feng shui.

We spent the night of August 4th, 1979, sleeping on the floor of our empty house, ready to begin our adventure the next day. Getting to sleep that night wasn't easy, and it wasn't just the anticipation of the next day—it was the weather. At dusk we stood on our deck and watched a tornado spin its way down the Mississippi—right toward us. And we had not yet closed the sale on the house. Fortunately for us, the funnel took a turn and missed us. Though the storm watch was over, neither of us got much sleep that night.

We finally started our journey west, but shortly after passing through Des Moines, the motorhome ground to a halt alongside the interstate. The transmission was kaput. We un-hooked the Honda Civic and, because cell phones hadn't yet been invented, drove to the nearest phone booth. We called AAMCO and they towed the motorhome back to Des Moines. When we picked it up and paid the bill, they gave us each a T-shirt that we kept for years, joking that they were the most expensive clothes we owned.

The first leg of our journey was completed the next day when we arrived at Dee's parents' home in Hastings. Her broth-er and family were visiting from California and, after a nice family reunion, our eleven-year-old niece joined us for the trip to the West Coast. We spent the next few weeks sightseeing our way across the West before putting Heather on a plane for home. Then, on our own, we spent nearly three months exploring, and falling in love with, the Pacific Northwest.

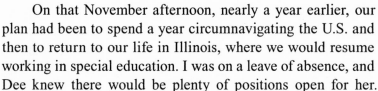

On that November afternoon, nearly a year earlier, our plan had been to spend a year circumnavigating the U.S. and then to return to our life in Illinois, where we would resume working in special education. I was on a leave of absence, and Dee knew there would be plenty of positions open for her. Now, with a household purge behind us and nearly a year to think about what we wanted to do, we weren't really sure we wanted to return to the Midwest, and it seemed there might be some new opportunities.

Staying in education in the Northwest was a possibility. Schools everywhere were desperate for folks trained in special education. An antique shop was briefly on our radar until friends in the business warned us that it might be fun but wasn't a very good prospect for earning a living. Then came the "aha." Didn't we love books? Wouldn't it be fun to spend all of our time around them? A college friend and I had once discussed opening a bookstore, but it had been largely a fantasy. Dee and I hadn't really talked about it since, but now it loomed as a possibility. What did we know about running a bookstore? Absolutely nothing.

We did both grow up as readers. From the time I encountered *Dick and Jane*, I was hooked on books. I checked them out from the school library, the city library, and even our church library. I was always enrolled in the library's summer reading program. And I loved getting books as presents. I don't remember a Christmas when I didn't receive at least a couple of books as gifts. In high school I read a lot of novels about sports, but I also remember reading *The Robe, The Light That Failed*, and Dr. Tom Dooley's books, among others.

My hometown didn't have a bookstore, and the drugstore had only a very limited supply of paperbacks, most of which were not appropriate for a young boy. I first began visiting bookstores regularly when I was in college, and I've haunted their aisles ever since.

Dee's brother, six years older, taught her to read before she went to school and she remembers, as a Kindergartner, getting to read to the first grade class. She, like I, treasured the books she received as gifts, since she also got many of her books from the library. Early reads for her included Nancy Drew books that, she believes, may have foreshadowed her current love of mysteries. In junior high she worked in the school library and often went to the local bookstore, which was small but packed with books. She read avidly through her high school years and headed off to college as an English major.

We both knew a lot about reading books. Now we set out to learn what we could about selling them by gathering material on small business and bookstores. *A Manual on Bookselling*, published by the American Booksellers Association, became our bible. Each of us must have read it cover-to-cover at least three times and often went back to it for specific information. Incidentally, a few years later, I wrote a chapter for a new edition of the book. We also read *Small Time Operator* by Bernard Kamoroff and *Honest Business* by Michael Phillips.

One book that we found inspirational was *Second Chance* by Herbert B. Livesey, a collection of personal accounts of people who left one career to pursue something new. Among the stories was one of a Wall Street broker who left the stress of the street and, with his wife, opened a bookstore in Vermont. Little did we suspect then that we would become friends with Ed and Barbara Morrow of Northshire Bookstore and later with their son Chris, who now runs the store. The world of bookselling is small and tight-knit.

We had made up our minds, and we began visiting every bookstore we could find, first in the Tacoma/Seattle area where we were encamped with friends, and later on a trip down the coast to Dee's brother's home in Southern California. Before we made the journey south, we made a list of criteria for the place we'd like to settle. We knew that we wanted to be located between the Canadian border and the San Francisco Bay area—Santa Rosa would be the last town we would consider. Though we had often visited Southern California, we had no desire to live there.

We were looking for a town with a population between 40,000 and 100,000 that was close enough to a larger city for its amenities but distant enough not to be primarily a haven for commuters. The town had to have a college or university, and it needed to be able to support a bookstore.

In one of the campgrounds earlier in our journey west, we serendipitously struck up a conversation with some folks whose motorhome had Washington plates.

"We're heading in your direction," we told them.

"Then don't miss Deception Pass and The Oyster Bar on Chuckanut Drive."

Before heading down to California, we took a short trip to Victoria via the Black Ball ferry from Port Angeles, returning on the Washington State Ferry to Anacortes. It was a sunny and warm September day as we headed back across the water with Mt. Baker in our sights much of the way. We've often wondered: If it had been a more typical Northwest day, would we have chosen to live here?

When we arrived in Anacortes, we called the Oyster Bar for reservations and learned we would have to wait three hours. That became the excuse for our first visit to Fairhaven. The historic district in the fall of 1979 was a much different place from today's. Only a handful of the businesses currently in the neighborhood were in existence then: Fairhaven Pharmacy, of course, had already been here for more than seventy years. Dos Padres was here, as were Gallery West, Fairhaven Bicycle, Tony's—which was roasting on-site at the time—Dirty Dan

Harris Restaurant, Good Earth Pottery, the Chimney Sweep, and Win's Drive-in. Of those businesses, only the bike shop, Gallery West, and Chimney Sweep have the same owners today.

Many of the other existing storefronts were empty, and several of the buildings one sees in Fairhaven today didn't yet exist, including of course the main Village Books building. There were also several businesses at the time that no longer exist, or have since moved, including the Food Coop—it was in the building now occupied by ArtWood—and The Picture Show, a small movie theater that was housed in the space that is now Fairhaven Runners. In spite of Fairhaven's less-than-thriving condition, we were charmed.

Brick buildings abounded and the remnants of streetcar tracks could still be seen in the middle of Harris Avenue. Tall turn-of-the-century storefronts reminded us of a much earlier era. And old-fashioned streetlights—recently added, we later learned—lined the streets

We were so enchanted by Fairhaven that we went back to spend a couple of days at Larrabee State Park and explore the entire area in more depth. One of those days we took a drive a bit further afield and discovered Wind & Tide Bookshop in Oak Harbor. We walked in to look around the store and were immediately struck by how inviting it was. The books were attractively displayed on the shelves and, in spite of its small size, the selection was great. It seemed apparent that each book had been carefully chosen.

We approached the couple behind the counter, who were about our age. "Hi, do you own the store?"

"Yes, we do," said the woman.

"How long have you had it?" asked Dee.

"Six weeks," she said.

We knew that we had to talk with these folks about their experience of buying, and now running, the bookstore. The conversation was so animated and compelling that Patti Pattee and Norman Sturdevant invited us home for dinner. We talked late into the evening about books and the book business, and we all felt a bond that would endure over the years.

Fairhaven, as well as the larger community of Bellingham, had scored high marks on our list of criteria, and with the bar set fairly high we headed south, visiting many communities along the way. We checked off Mount Vernon—it already had a great bookstore. Scott's was then located in the mall but was anything but a "mall" store. Mary Scott and her family later became good friends, and thinking now about the demise of that bookstore still makes us sad.

One by one we checked off potential towns—Olympia, Salem, Corvalis, Eugene, Eureka, Napa, Sonoma, and finally Santa Rosa.

Our scouting mission complete, we headed south to visit Dee's brother and family. We continued to visit bookstores on the way, looking for ideas but no longer considering places to locate. We arrived in Southern California a couple of weeks before Christmas and stayed until early February. It wasn't difficult to make the decision, based on our evaluation of the places we'd visited, to return to Bellingham and open a bookstore. So we spent our time reading about business and brainstorming ideas about the store until heading back north.

On February 20, 1980, Bellingham became our new home. We stayed at Larrabee State Park until we found a southside apartment, then we began searching for a location for the store. Although our hearts were set on Fairhaven, much of the property had been optioned by one developer who was working on larger prospects and was not particularly interested in renting to a startup business. In spite of several empty storefronts, there were few spaces truly available at the time, so we looked a little farther afield. Finding nothing that suited us elsewhere in the area, we came back to more closely explore Fairhaven. We homed in on the train car on the corner of Mill and 12th Street—the train cars that would be removed in the fall of 2009. We contacted the owner, carefully measured the space, and began drawing up plans for the store.

"Did it always do this?" I asked. "Did it turn brown every winter?"

Dee just laughed. During our exploration of the book business we had discovered that the American Booksellers Association conducted Prospective Bookseller Schools, and after signing up for their next school, we were driving back to the Midwest in late March. We had swapped our Honda Civic for Norman and Patti's van so we could pick up our stored possessions.

It was the midst of a recession. Interest rates hit 20% on the second of April, and Robert Hale, then President of the American Booksellers Association, welcomed us to Prospective Booksellers School.

"I don't know if I'm looking at fifty of the bravest people I've ever seen or fifty of the craziest," said Hale. It was likely some combination of the two.

The course was packed with information about all aspects of the book business, from philosophical questions about books one would or would not stock, to the nitty gritty details of how to keep track of inventory. We talked about financial management, book buying, marketing, customer service... even color preferences in retail. Because Dee and I had read the *Manual on Bookselling* and talked with so many booksellers, we had some understanding of the basics of the business and were prepared to absorb much of the detail.

That wasn't the case for one couple who had come from Houston. In one of the first sessions, before we got to financial management, an instructor made a passing reference to the average book discount to retailers—40% at that time.

"Excuse me," said the woman from Houston, "did you say 40%? Do you mean we would pay $6 for a book we would sell for $10?"

"Wholesale discounts do vary," said the instructor, "but that is the average."

"How are we going to get rich at that rate?"

From the look on the instructor's face, it was clear that getting rich was not in the cards. Fortunately, we knew the basic business model and hadn't chosen bookselling to get rich, at least not in the monetary sense.

Among the many things we learned at the school that helped determine our path forward, two in particular stand out. First, when we showed the instructors the plans for the train car, they dismissed them immediately.

"What will you do if you're successful?" asked one instructor. "Where will you have room to expand?"

We didn't have a good answer.

Second, we had decided to call the store The Village Book Shoppe. We likely would have chosen Fairhaven Books, but when Phil and Linda Magruder moved their shop from the Marketplace in Fairhaven to downtown, about a year and a half before our arrival, they had taken the name with them.

One evening, sitting in the bar with the instructors after the day's sessions, one of the instructors asked, "What are you going to call your store?"

"The Village Book Shoppe," Dee said.

"Well, I hope that doesn't have two p's and an e on the end," she said. "That's just too cute."

Those two pieces of advice might not have been worth the cost of the course, but we also left the school with reams of notes and ideas, even more determined to launch the store. We stopped in Illinois to pick up the rest of our worldly possessions and headed back to Washington.

We had lots of work to do. Now convinced that the train car was a bad idea, we had to search harder for a location. We learned that Gary Imus, the nephew of one of Fairhaven's major property owners, Ken Imus, was running a kitchen shop called Country Corner. Gary had expanded his business to carry furniture and had used the entire space of the building. But since the idea may have been ahead of its time, he'd been forced to pull back and nearly half the building space, just under 1500 square feet, was available to rent. We snapped it up.

It was an interesting space, divided down the middle by a wall that stopped far short of the high ceilings. There were arched openings at the front leading into each space and a couple of open doorways along the length of the dividing wall. The two businesses would be quite open into one another, and we even planned to face our cookbook section toward one of the openings into the kitchen shop.

We had decided that we wanted to begin our business with good relationships in the community, so we set out to introduce ourselves to Phil and Linda at Fairhaven Books in downtown Bellingham.

"Hi, we're Chuck and Dee Robinson," I said. "We think Bellingham is big enough to support another independent bookstore and we plan to open one."

"We agree," said Phil. "Where do you plan to open?"

"Fairhaven," Dee said.

Phil and Linda were not keen on our choice of location. They had been in the Marketplace building (now called Sycamore Square) for several years, first on an upper floor and then on the main floor, and they thought they had made a good choice in moving downtown. We, on the other hand, had talked with many folks who missed having a bookstore in Fairhaven and who admitted that they seldom ventured downtown. In spite of our differences of opinion about location, we did set the foundation for a positive business relationship that continued until they closed their store nearly five years later, after their children were grown and they had decided to move on to other ventures. We valued them as book business colleagues and now value them as customers.

Much of the three months between the time we returned to Bellingham and opening the store on June 20 was a blur of activity. We liked a shelf design from a shop on the Oregon coast and, using materials that had been salvaged from one of the last buildings of the PAF cannery at the end of Harris Avenue, we built our own shelves for the store. Though neither of us would ever be considered handy, we undertook ripping full dimension lumber to the sizes we needed, building jigs on the floor so that the shelving was consistent, then stained and, in the case of the children's area shelves, painted the fixtures.

Our friends Norman and Patti continued to mentor us, answering innumerable questions and giving sage advice. On the morning of May 18, 1980, we were sitting at their dining room table in their home on the West Beach of Whidbey Island. We were reviewing a projected opening order and they were suggesting increases or decreases in the numbers based on where they thought that book was in its life cycle. Just after 8:30 we heard a loud explosion. Familiar with sonic booms from the Naval Air Station, they knew it wasn't one. Since they had been having work done on their roof that week, Patti and I ran outdoors to look at the roof. No clues there. Mystified, but with lots of work still to be done, we went back inside and resumed reviewing the order.

We worked through the afternoon and into the evening, when Dee and I drove back to Bellingham. We talked all the way home, in part because we had much to discuss about the store, but also because we had no radio in the van. We reached home exhausted and immediately crawled into bed. The next morning Dee got up first and turned on the TV, then rushed into the bedroom.

"Chuck, wake up," she said. "Do you know what that was we heard yesterday?"

I shook my head.

"It was Mt. Saint Helens erupting."

At the time, we recognized the eruption as a huge natural phenomenon and a major disaster for many living near the mountain, including the families of the fifty-seven people who lost their lives. We made no association with the book business. But within weeks of opening the store, books about the eruption became bestsellers. *Mount St. Helens: A Changing Landscape* by Chuck Williams was number three on our hardcover bestseller list that first year, and *Volcano: The Eruption of Mount St. Helens* by the combined staffs of *The Longview Daily News* and *The Bellevue Journal-American* was number three on the softcover bestseller list. The latter received a rave review in the *New York Times* and stayed on the *NYT* bestseller list for several weeks. One of the reporters from the Longview paper, William Dietrich, went on to become an award-winning Northwest author and a good friend.

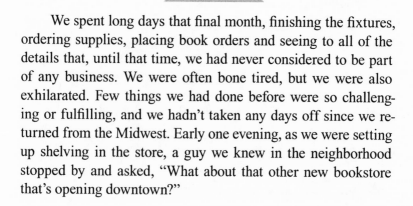

We spent long days that final month, finishing the fixtures, ordering supplies, placing book orders and seeing to all of the details that, until that time, we had never considered to be part of any business. We were often bone tired, but we were also exhilarated. Few things we had done before were so challenging or fulfilling, and we hadn't taken any days off since we returned from the Midwest. Early one evening, as we were setting up shelving in the store, a guy we knew in the neighborhood stopped by and asked, "What about that other new bookstore that's opening downtown?"

"What?" We both gasped. "Where?"

"On Grand Avenue," he said. "I think it's called Northern Lights Bookstore."

Dee and I raced to our van and drove downtown. There, working on the same things we had been working on in Fairhaven, was Greg Oldham, preparing to open a new bookstore. We knocked on the door, introduced ourselves, and told Greg what we were up to. Fortunately, even though we would be competitors, our common interests and goals helped us form a bond that continued until Greg closed his store two years later and went to law school.

We were expecting our largest order of books to arrive on Friday, June 13. All of the shelves were set, and our plan was to get the books displayed and open the store early the next week. The book order didn't arrive on Friday, and it felt a little bit like being all dressed up with nowhere to go. But we found a place to go—the Deming Logging Show. It was a great getaway for us and a chance to see part of the area we hadn't yet explored.

When the boxes of books arrived the next week we set about getting the store ready. It seemed to us that we had a huge number of books, but some time later a good customer shared her thoughts from those first days.

"I wasn't sure you'd make it," Nell said. "Even with all those single copies faced out, the books barely covered the shelves. I didn't think you could sell enough books to stay in business."

We opened the store on Friday, June 20, 1980. It was an auspicious time for bookstores in Bellingham. Not only had Greg opened Northern Lights earlier that week, but a metaphysical bookstore called Akasha opened as well. Our long journey had truly begun.

Chapter 2

Getting Going & Settling In 1980–1984

Author events, we decided early in our planning for the bookstore, would be a central offering and a way to market our store. Three weeks after opening, we hosted our first, when James Stewart Thayer came on Sunday afternoon, July 13, to sign *The Earhart Betrayal*. This was truly a book signing, before the popularity of author readings or talks.

No one in Bellingham had been regularly holding author events, and there seemed to be a pent-up demand. We sold twenty copies of a brand new hardcover novel from a relatively unknown author. We thought we'd struck pay dirt. Though every event since then has not gone as swimmingly, we look back with great pleasure at the thousands of events we've held over the years.

Ivan Doig was already a regional celebrity and had received national attention when he appeared at the store in late November of 1980 for his new book *Winter Brothers*. His first book, *This House of Sky*, had enchanted reviewers from coast to coast and prompted the *Washington Star* to say, "Mr. Doig's sense of the land and his marvelous sensitivity to the lives that touched his own make *This House of Sky* a work of art." It also earned him nominations for the National Book Award and Pulitzer Prize. Ivan has become a friend and has appeared at the store for each of his books since then.

That first summer, we had sent Tom Robbins a note inviting him to sign his forthcoming book *Still Life With Woodpecker*. In late July Tom responded, "We can try to shoot for a Sunday in early December, if that suits you." It certainly suited us, and a later postcard—sporting a '50s Chevy and a fake rocket—said, with obvious reference to Pearl Harbor, "Okay, let's shoot for Dec. 7 and hope it doesn't bomb."

It began snowing in earnest the evening of December 6th and continued into the morning of the 7th with little promise of letting up. Though we didn't open until noon on Sundays in those days, Dee and I stayed near the phone that morning and answered a deluge of calls:

"Is Tom Robbins still coming?" was the unremitting refrain.

"Yes, he'll be here at noon," we said to each caller, hoping that the roads from LaConner didn't make liars of us.

Late in the morning, picking up the ringing phone, fully prepared to say, "Yes, Tom Robbins is coming," I heard, in a recognizable Carolina drawl, "Should I still come?"

"YES!" I said.

"Okay, I'll be there by noon."

The signing was a great success. Bellinghamsters, undaunted by the several inches of snow that blanketed the town, turned out in great numbers to talk with Tom and buy his latest book. The event even merited a front page photo and story in that Monday's *Bellingham Herald*. We were thrilled, but wondered if it had just been a slow-news weekend.

At an after-event dinner, John Wright, one of our booksellers at the time, asked Tom, "Do people ever ask you to sign strange things in their books?"

"All the time," Tom said. "In fact, just today a woman asked me to sign the book to 'the woman who inspired this novel.'"

"What did you do?"

"I signed it, 'to a woman who I understand inspires novels'"

Tom Robbins had a well-earned reputation for signing anything anyone put in front of him. It didn't have to be one of his books. At that first signing we watched him autograph a Swahili dictionary. But several years later the habit came back to haunt him. At an event in Seattle he was asked by several folks to sign a book called *fuck YES* by Reverend Wing F. Fing M.D., Ph.D., L.L.D., D.V.D., and much, much more!

Because of the style in which the book was written and the obvious use of a nom de plume, many suspected Robbins was the author. He was not. But Tom, in his usual manner, signed the books. A short time later I received a call.

"Chuck, I'm being sued for trading on this guy's fame," Tom said.

"That's ridiculous," I said. "You're a bestselling author, and nobody knows who this guy is."

"Would you tell my attorney that?"

"Of course," I said. "Have her call me."

I never heard from Tom's attorney, and mentioned it when I saw him a few months later.

"Well, we settled out of court," Tom said. "And if it hadn't cost so much money this would all be very funny." I suspect he is much more cautious about what he signs now.

Tom returned to Village Books four years later to sign *Jitterbug Perfume*—also in December, but this time without the blizzard. He spent unlimited time with each fan, just as he had at his first signing and as he generously does with each new book.

Blizzards are not the only hazards that have caused anxiety with author events in those early years. In the summer of 1981 we were excited to have Jean Auel coming to sign the new paperback edition of her big bestseller *The Clan of the Cave Bear*. As we ticked off the days leading up to the signing, we became increasingly nervous that the books had not yet arrived, so I called the publisher.

"That's a super release," said the voice on the other end of the line. "It can't be shipped yet."

"But we have the author signing here next Saturday."

"Sorry, that's the rule. If it's a super release we can't make an exception."

In desperation I called the publicity department. They, after all, had set up the signing. After a bit of explaining we were able to get the books released, but only after a Vice President of Bantam signed off. Disaster was averted once again. The signing went well, though within a couple of weeks, after *The Clan of the Cave Bear* hit the national bestseller lists, we were selling more copies of the book each Saturday than we did the day of the signing.

Jean returned in November of 1982 to sign the second in her "Earth's Children" series, *The Valley of Horses*. Then, it seemed, she followed the habits of the cave bear and hibernated for some time to write the next book, which was delayed by more than a year past its planned publication date. Others in the promised six-book series were likewise delayed and, at this writing—nearly thirty years after the publication of the first book—no date has been set for the final installment.

"What the hell is a non-buyer?" asked the vendor as he stared at our badges.

On the advice of a bookstore owner we had visited, we were at the gift show at Seattle Center shortly before opening the store. Only established businesses were allowed to buy merchandise, so we had been given these unusual badges to alert vendors not to sell to us.

"Well, being a non-buyer doesn't separate you from most of the other folks here," the vendor responded.

I guess the recession had taken a toll on his business as well.

We knew from our bookstore visits and our time at booksellers schools that we needed to carry some merchandise other than books. Cards and gifts were commonly offered in most bookstores, but the variety of items at this show, from cheap souvenirs to luxury home decor, was overwhelming. We stuffed bags with handouts from dozens of booths and lugged our finds back home to sort out our favorites.

In the first few months we carried a small offering of greeting cards, a selection of rubber stamps, backgammon and chess sets, some pens and assorted writing papers, puzzles, posters, calendars, some bookmarks, and a few other miscellaneous "sidelines" as they are often called in the book business. As we continued to add to these offerings, we were faced with a problem and an opportunity.

The problem was twofold. We would soon run out of room for more non-book items in the store, and we didn't want the bookstore atmosphere to be diluted by other merchandise. We also recognized an opportunity in the advent of alternative card and paper stores. From Seattle to Eugene, we had seen evidence of this new trend in a business that had been dominated by Hallmark and Gibson. Our entrepreneurial juices began to flow.

On one of our early visits to Bellingham we had met JoAnn Hanesworth in her candy store on the main floor of the Marketplace building. In 1981 she had moved the store downtown, then sold it in early 1982. We had immediately taken a liking to JoAnn and admired the way she ran her store, so we called her and asked if she would meet us at the Fairhaven Restaurant. Over lunch we laid out our idea for opening a card, paper, and gift store. She listened intently and asked a few questions.

"Would you like to help us open the store and be our manager?" Dee asked.

"I don't know anything about greeting cards," JoAnn said.

"Neither do we," I admitted.

JoAnn thought the prospect sounded interesting, but said she would have to talk with her husband about it. Don was working in the oil fields of Alaska at the time. When they next talked on the phone, he became so distracted talking with their son about his high school football game that the subject never came up. JoAnn made the decision on her own and called us back to say she would like to give it a try. That was great news for us.

Once again, choosing a location was on the top of our list. Because the bookstore had been successful and we had continued to add books, we were in need of more space. So in late September of 1982 we moved Village Books a couple of buildings south, into a space in the Knights of Pythias building that had been vacant for several years. We closed the store on a Saturday evening and reopened on Monday morning in the new space. Dee talked about that move in a newspaper article about Village Books: "Though it wasn't far to move," she said, "anyone who has moved their own book collection probably has some appreciation for the task."

For our Grand Reopening Celebration in the new location, we held a signing with *Herman* cartoonist Jim Unger. Our store cat found a welcoming spot on Jim's lap and remained for more than two hours while he signed books. For several years following the event, when we saw Jim at our national conventions, he would ask about Athena. Named after the Goddess of Wisdom by customer Pete Stark in a naming contest, Athena continued to live at the store for six years before retiring to live a long life in the country.

After getting the bookstore reopened, we prepared for the opening of the card and gift shop in the space that was Village Books. Once again our friends Norman and Patti had a strong influence in our business decisions, and while we were planning the new store we went back to Oak Harbor to talk with them about the project. Over dinner, and who knows how many bottles of wine, we brainstormed names for the store. To this day we're uncertain who came up with the final name—

that may be because of the wine—but we think it was Norman who shouted out, "Paper Dreams." It stuck, and in October we opened the new store. Dee had long been infatuated with penguins, so we adopted one for the logo.

Between 1982 and 1985, Paper Dreams went through some significant changes, first with shifts in our space-sharing neighbors, next with a second location, and finally as the shop itself expanded. After Village Books moved into its new space, Country Corner moved into the vacant storefront just to the north of us and Fabrications—as the name would suggest, a fabric store—opened in the space Country Corner vacated. Before long, Gary closed his store, and in November of 1984, Bill Osborn moved his Aero Marine Ice Cream Parlor from State Street into that space.

Less than a year after opening Paper Dreams, we were approached to open a second location of Village Books in Yew Street Center, at the corner of Yew Street and Alabama. From talking with friends in the book business who had expanded their businesses in that way, we had learned of the difficulties inherent in operating a second location of a bookstore, particularly in a town the size of Bellingham. So we said no. However, Bob and Dan Barr, the father and son team who represented the center, were persistent. We still resisted, until one day we got a call from Dan.

"Chuck, we'd really like to have you in this center," he said.

"I'm sorry," I said, "but Dee and I have talked it over, and having a second bookstore just won't work for us."

"Well then," he said, "how about a second Paper Dreams location with a bookstore component?"

"Gee, Dan, I'm sorry," I said, "I just don't think that would work, either."

After a few more minutes of continued urging, which I

continued to resist, Dan thanked me for considering the possibility and we hung up. In just a few minutes the phone rang again.

"Chuck, this is Bob Barr. Dan said I should call you and tell you what we're prepared to do."

Bob explained a very attractive rent arrangement, based on a percentage of sales only, with only a year commitment. They had taken nearly all of the risk out of the venture. The deal, as Bob had likely suspected, was just too good to pass up, and in November of 1983 we opened a second location of Paper Dreams—with a large book section—in a big, new storefront at the south end of Yew Street Center.

I'd love to be able to say that it was a great success, but given that it no longer exists, that is obviously not the case. One of our assumptions in opening the second location was that we would be able to split inventory orders between the two stores because of the minimum quantity of cards and other products we were required to buy. In theory that was a great idea. In practice it didn't work so well. It had never occurred to us that two locations, only four miles apart, could have such different markets. Some products that we couldn't keep on the shelves in Fairhaven didn't sell at all at Yew Street, and vice versa. We had to think quite differently about the two stores. And, with only two stores, no other economies of scale were achieved. Instead of being able to take care of two stores in just a bit more time than one, it felt like it more than doubled the workload.

Shopping patterns were also quite different. In Fairhaven our busiest days had always been the weekends. The area was, after all, a destination. At Yew Street the store served as a convenient place to stop on the way to and from other destinations. We should have suspected that from the other successful businesses already located there—a pharmacy, a cleaners, a 7-11, and a bakery. Saturdays were nearly dead, as folks went to other shopping areas… like Fairhaven.

That first holiday season was moderately successful, and

we had planned that the business would grow after the first of the year. It didn't. Faced with making buying decisions for the next holiday season—something that takes place much earlier in the year than non-retail folks would ever suspect—and needing to make a decision about renewing our lease, we pondered closing the store at the end of our contract in November, never a wise time to close a retail store. We contacted Dan Barr and explained our dilemma.

"Instead of renewing your lease, why don't we just extend it on a month to month basis," Dan said. "You can see how you do in a second holiday season and then make a decision."

We agreed and went forward planning and buying for a second holiday season. Unfortunately, the season showed no improvement over the previous holiday, and we had not had much improvement during the year. We called Dan after Christmas.

"I'm sorry, Dan, but this just isn't going to work for us," I said.

"We're sorry, too, but you did give it your best shot. Thanks for giving it a try."

We've been very fortunate in all of our landlord relationships, but it would be difficult to imagine nicer or more accommodating folks to work with than the Barrs. Dan even called several years later with a bookstore opportunity east of the Cascades. It didn't fit what we wanted to do, but once again we had a pleasant conversation. The Yew Street experience, though unsuccessful, provided some fairly inexpensive lessons about retail—the importance of location, that micro markets exist within larger markets, and that economies of scale are very difficult to achieve in small organizations. It allowed us to face, much more realistically, the many opportunities we would be offered over the coming years.

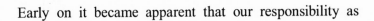

Early on it became apparent that our responsibility as

booksellers included involvement in the issues of censorship and privacy. Our friend Joyce Meskis of The Tattered Cover in Denver once wondered, because of the number of issues that arose here, if there was a big censorship magnet located in Bellingham. Though it may, at times, have seemed so, censorship and privacy concerns occur everywhere. Village Books has been involved, directly and tangentially, in a number of those issues.

I have often wondered where the conservatives were when it came to defending free speech. It seems that the first amendment is the most conservative part of the U.S. Constitution, yet when there are issues involving censorship, it's often conservatives on the attack. Occasionally there's an exception.

A controversy arose at WWU around selling *Playboy* magazine on campus. The student association held a forum and asked me to be on the panel with Dan Larner, who served on the ACLU state board. Mark Nelson, a county leader of the Republican party, and Cathy Mickels, head of the Washington Alliance of Families and a national board member and state leader of the Eagle Forum, were also invited.

Dan and I, predictably, argued for freedom of access to materials, and Cathy Mickels railed against the magazine being sold on campus. For many, the surprise came when the mic was passed to Mark Nelson. He held up a Victorian erotic novel and said, "This is what I like, and I don't want anyone telling me what I should or should not read."

It was during these early years that Dee and I first became intermeshed in the fabric of the local community. Our first involvement was right in our own neighborhood, with the Old Fairhaven Association. Many believe this to be an area merchant group, but its function goes far beyond into area beautification and the preservation of Fairhaven's historic character, with the merchant committee just one part of the organization. I served on the board and as the president of OFA in the early 1980s.

Dee joined the board of Northwest Women's Services, an organization that oversaw counseling for women, and I was appointed to the county's mental health board. Our experiences helped us develop a much better understanding of the social network and the importance of developing and supporting community organizations.

This was also when we began to engage with the larger community of booksellers. Because our experience at booksellers school had been so positive, and believing that the experiences of a relatively new bookseller could be helpful to others, I volunteered to teach at future ABA booksellers schools. I taught in the spring of 1982 and was a faculty member of nearly every prospective school for the next decade.

Those schools were intended, as much as anything, to give folks basic information to help them decide if they wanted to pursue owning a bookstore. We considered the school experience to be just as successful—maybe more so—if a person decided not to go forward.

Potential bookstore owners came from all walks of life– lawyers, accountants, teachers, housewives, and retirees–and all economic circumstances from near poverty level to independently wealthy. Each was looking for a good picture of what it was like to own a bookstore, and what it might take to be successful. Very few had extensive business experience–the book business tends to attract dreamers, not pragmatists.

In a final session of one school, I was nearly attacked by a gentleman who thought I was withholding the "secret formula" for a successful bookstore. He was certain I was making money hand over fist, and just didn't want to share how to do it.

At another school, as a number of us were relaxing in the bar one evening, a very wealthy woman expressed some doubts about opening the store she had planned. It seemed to many of us that she was more interested in telling her friends that she owned a bookstore than she was in running one.

"I just don't know whether I can afford this," she said.

In those days I knew off the top of my head the costs of opening a store, and I ran through them with her—so much for leasehold improvements, this much for fixtures, another amount for equipment, a figure for inventory, etc. When finished, I mentioned the total amount, about $250,000.

"Suppose you spent that much money, then locked the doors and walked away," I said. "Could you afford to lose that much?"

"Yes."

"Then what's the question?" I asked.

She was speechless, realizing, I suspect, her own motivations for having a bookstore and pondering the value.

Many people who attended the schools at which I taught were far more serious in their intent and went on to open successful bookstores. Among them are Carla Cohen of Politics and Prose in Washington, D.C.; Roger Page of Island Books on Mercer Island; Carol Santoro, who first opened Second Story Books and now owns Santoro's Books in Seattle; Priscilla Ulene and Harriet Bay, who opened and have since sold Traveler's Bookcase in Los Angeles; Keebe Fitch of McIntyre's Books in Fearrington Village, North Carolina; and Barry Martin, who owns Book'em Mysteries in Pasadena.

It was a logical step from teaching at the schools to serving on the ABA education committee. Dee also began teaching at the schools, and joined the education committee several years later.

We began attending meetings of the Pacific Northwest Booksellers Association, an organization that serves booksellers in the states of Washington, Oregon, Idaho, Montana, and Alaska. Within a short time I was elected to that board.

The concentric circles of our community involvement continued to broaden and, though our lives became much busier, they also became much richer.

While I was teaching at a prospective booksellers school in Berkeley in 1984, I got a phone call from Dee, who was back home minding the store.

"Gary Larson is sick and can't come to the signing this afternoon," she said. "What am I going to say to the people who show up?"

"Oh my gosh, maybe you should call the publisher and get a new date so you can tell folks when he will be there," I said.

"Good idea. I'll call you back."

I waited anxiously, hoping that Dee would be able to reach the right person and get a new date set before adoring fans of Larson's *The Far Side* showed up that afternoon. I didn't have to wait long.

"He's coming," was all she said.

"When?"

"Today."

"Today? What happened?"

"When I told the publisher that Gary had cancelled, he said 'Let me call you right back,'" she told me. "And he did. He said Gary would be here today."

Apparently, Gary was feeling incredible pressure to finish his daily panels and promote his latest book at the same time. He is also painfully shy, and I suspect the "illness" he was suffering due to these pressures may have been temporarily cured with a call from his publisher. The signing went well. Gary was gracious, and fans were thrilled. But it is possible that his unease in promoting his books is, in part, what led him to give up the cartoon business altogether—to the chagrin of his many fans, including us.

Before Dee and I decided to open the bookstore, we were clear that whatever we pursued as a career had to allow for vacations and travel. We never have subscribed to the theory that one should work his or her entire life, then retire to live. We had heard far too many stories about folks being incapacitated or dying shortly after retirement. We had also heard many business owners complain that they had worked for years and years and never taken a vacation. We thought, "What's the point?"

So we opened the store in full agreement that we would travel and, if it didn't work for the business, we would find another line of work. Less than a year after we opened, we attended the ABA Convention in Atlanta. Eastern Airlines (remember them?) was offering a special three-week, fly-anywhere package at one low price that was less than a round-trip ticket to Atlanta.

We left Seattle and flew to Omaha—through Atlanta, oddly enough—where we rented a car and drove to Hastings to visit Dee's parents. We then flew from Omaha to Atlanta for the convention and trade show.

When we first looked out over the trade show floor from the second floor viewing area we were stunned. "Oh my god," I said. Spread out below us in a space the size of eight football fields were more than 1500 booths of books. We would soon see nearly every publisher we had ever heard of, and many we hadn't.

We would also see authors John Irving, Arthur Ashe, Garry Trudeau, Fanny Flagg, and Judy Blume, among others. At an author breakfast, Harry Reasoner introduced Eudora Welty by telling a story about being on assignment with newsman Hughes Rudd.

"We were sitting in a bar late one night when I turned to Hughes and asked, 'What do you want to be when you grow up?' Hughes replied, 'I want to be as good a writer as Eudora Welty.'"

The look on Eudora Welty's face was one of astonishment. It was a charmingly naive response from a woman who thought of herself as just a little old lady from Jackson, Mississippi, who wrote short stories.

In an article about the convention, *The New York Times*

said, "What's the spirit of the trade as A.B.A. '81 opens? With travel costs high, with sales 'flat' and the economy wobbly, publishers, booksellers and agentry in all its forms seem to be keeping their fingers crossed."

Perhaps it was our naivete or the afterglow of the convention, but with bags stuffed with books and publisher's giveaway t-shirts, smiles on our faces, we flew to St. Martin with our bookselling friends Norman and Patti to spend a week in the Caribbean before heading back to work.

When we returned to Bellingham, Abbe Rolnick, our first and only employee at the time, was a little frazzled, but there were no major crises. The store had survived and sold books, and there wasn't even much clean-up to do.

We were refreshed and relaxed, and coming from a convention and a week with other booksellers, we were full of ideas. We took this as a sign.

When asked to name their biggest problem, many business owners say it's the people who work for them. We've never felt that way. That's not to say there are no difficulties with staff or that we don't get frustrated with people at times (or they with us). However, the people who have worked with us over the years have brought us far more joy than sorrow. In small business, the relationships between owners and those who work in the business is complicated, and business "experts" often warn against becoming friends with employees or creating a "family" atmosphere. Not only have we found that impossible, we believe it's undesirable. We've watched people who came to us as young students mature and raise families and, regretfully, we've seen more than one pass away.

It was just the two of us—Dee and I—when we opened the store. In our first month we met a young woman who had recently moved to Bellingham from Puerto Rico, where she had owned a bookstore. Abbe was originally from the East Coast, but had met and married a man whose family owned one of the largest Puerto Rican coffee companies. When they divorced, she sold the store and came to the Northwest, where she had college friends, to start a new life.

Dee's parents had announced they would be coming to visit us in August. Though I would be working the store most of the time they were here, while Dee spent time with them, we knew that we would like to visit some sites together and wanted to have one day off. So, we asked Abbe if we could hire her to run the store for a day. She said yes, and when we were ready to hire our first employee later that fall, she was our choice. Abbe stayed with us for several years, becoming our first children's book buyer, until she went off to start her own native plant business. Thirty years later, she has raised three kids, was the CEO of Cascade DAFO, and now owns two Robeks stores in Bellingham. Abbe contributed much in the early days of the store, and we love running into her at community events and catching up on her life.

Our first year in business had exceeded our sales expectations by seventy percent and sales had grown each year since. Now, with nearly half a decade of Village Books under our belts, we were beginning to feel established. The staff had grown to half a dozen, including Krista Hunter who joined us in 1983 and would stay with the store for the next twenty-four years. But some big changes were about to happen.

Chapter 3

The Go Go Years 1985–1990

When independent booksellers allude to "the good old days," we're likely talking about the mid-'80s. It was a time of seemingly unbounded growth. The mall-based chain stores had opened in nearly all of their potential locations, Bellingham being one of the few exceptions, and year-to-year sales were seeing double-digit increases.

It was during this time that bookstores, including Village Books, began to add computerized inventory systems and, though some thought they made the profession less genteel, they certainly helped us better serve our customers. We had a couple of self-described luddites on staff who were, at first, quite reluctant about our computerization. Ironically, a year later, on one of the rare occasions when the computer system crashed, they were the ones who felt lost without the computers. Today it's hard to imagine what we would do without them.

Another phenomenon had begun to take root in bookstores. From coast to coast, cafés were being added. Elliott Bay in Seattle was one of the early adopters, along with Kramer Books in Washington, D.C. with their aptly named café, Afterwords. We also admired the creativity of Oxford Books in Atlanta (no longer in existence) when they named their café Cup and Chaucer.

In the late spring of 1985 we learned that Aero Marine Ice Cream Parlor would be moving back to State Street, and the wheels began to turn in our heads. We were, again, beginning to feel a bit cramped in our space, and the idea of adding a bookstore café had strong appeal.

Our friends Ray and Taimi Dunn had owned a chain of pizza parlors they had recently sold, and Ray, with extensive experience in food service, was considering his options. We had often fantasized with them about a bookstore café, so we approached them about actually doing that in part of the space that the ice cream parlor had occupied. We would open up the wall into the bookstore and take the area behind the café as additional bookstore space. They liked the idea.

Taimi, Ray, Dee and I brainstormed names (likely over several glasses of wine) that would be fitting for a bookstore café. Ultimately we came up with Colophon Café. Because of the abundance of cow items that Taimi later added to the café, folks often think that colophon refers to something bovine. The reference is actually far more literary.

In addition to the Greek-derived meaning of "summit, finishing touch or last word," colophon has two publishing references. First, it's the publisher's logo on a book, such as Bantam's rooster, Knopf's borzoi or Pocketbooks' kangaroo. The second refers to a page at the end of the book that includes information about the book's design and typography.

But Tom Billings may have thought his first day on the job was more fitting for a dairy farm than a bookstore with a café. Rather than shelving books or helping customers find good reads, he was swinging a sledge hammer, removing the wall between the bookstore and new café area. While he didn't seem to mind the task, I suspect that he wished he hadn't partied quite so heartily the night before. Tom continued to work at the store for several years, and a quote in one of our newsletters likely explains why:

"It's an awfully swell place to work because most days not

much is taken too seriously. This leaves me energy in my spare time for more solemn pursuits—basketball and the creation of unpublishable short stories."

The ice cream parlor had vacated the space at the end of June, and the Colophon Café held its Grand Opening on Village Books' fifth anniversary, Sunday, July 20, 1985, with locally-made Far-Far's ice cream and a special blend of coffee roasted just across the street at Tony's. The Colophon's menu quickly expanded from ice cream and coffee to bagels, salads, sand-wiches, chowder and soups, including their famous (and still extremely popular) African Peanut soup, named in honor of the film *Out of Africa*, which won the 1985 Oscar for Best Picture.

The Colophon Café has gone on to be one of the longest-operating, most successful restaurants in Northwest Washington, and its reputation has spread far and wide. Chris Brainard and Dave Killian joined the Colophon in the '90s and, after working there for a number of years, became partners, then full owners.

By the mid-'80s our author program had become fairly well established, with three or four events each quarter, pro-moted with terrific posters created by local artist Jane Burns. So we turned our attention to another type of author event.

Early 1986 was a time when the cable companies felt some obligation to the local community, and independent producer James Trotter approached us about sponsoring and helping to create a program about books. We jumped at the chance, and over the course of two seasons created sixty-one half-hour epi-sodes of "The Reading Room." Many of the guests were region-al authors, including Ivan Doig, Laura Kalpakian, Jo Dereske, and W.P. Kinsella. Others, nationally famous and not from the area, included L.S.D. guru Timothy Leary, NFL quarterback Kenny "Snake" Stabler, *Das Boot* screenwriter Ronald Cohen, and *Washington Post* correspondent George Wilson.

Our Spring 1986 newsletter, *The Village Voice*, said this about first-season host, Greg Cornia: "The ease with which he moves and talks suggests that television is something he has done for years. In fact, when "The Reading Room" takes its summer hiatus in mid-June, Greg will have only twenty-one shows 'in the can.'" Poet Robert Huff expressed obvious surprise when Greg referenced a poem from his first book, published many years earlier. Author John Miles appeared on the program with the original publication of *Koma Kulshan* (our Chuckanut Editions imprint has recently published a revised and expanded edition). Having appeared on numerous radio and television programs for the book, Miles pronounced Greg's interview his best and praised his preparation as outstanding.

In the second season, Ron Hardesty—the lawyer/musician who has since provided musical entertainment on the "Chuckanut Radio Hour"—took the reins as host and continued the tradition of professionalism. *Seattle Times* television columnist John Voorhees wrote that "The Reading Room" had "an excellent series of interviews," and called it "the kind of program that shows up the shallowness of the bulk of TV's treatment of authors." Mary Marvin, writing for *The Post*, quoted LA-based freelance journalist Ric Gentry talking about his appearance on the program:

"I'm usually the one asking the questions. But what I found most impressive was how technically sophisticated and professional were my hosts and the crew at Channel 10. They were as adept and creative as any outfit I've visited in LA or other large cities. James Trotter behind the camera and Ron Hardesty in front of it are as astute at what they do as you'll probably find anywhere."

During its first season "The Reading Room" was broadcast to 21,000 local viewers and, due to its popularity, was picked that fall by Group W Cable in Seattle and made available to 350,000 subscribers. Unfortunately, the days of cable's interest in airing local programs disappeared as quickly as it had begun, and the program ended after the second season.

In 1985, after serving on the board of the Pacific Northwest Booksellers Association for about three years, I became the organization's president. I learned much from my colleagues in the Northwest and also had the opportunity to meet and learn from other regional leaders from around the country. After my term ended in 1987, I joined the board of the American Booksellers Association (ABA). It's hard to measure the value of these associations to our business and to us personally, with the many opportunities they have presented us—among them the chance to meet some very interesting and well-known people.

One morning a few years ago, while reading the newspaper, I was struck with how unusual my life has been. A short article reported an interview with Tom Hanks. The reporter suggested to Hanks that the public always hears about the downside of celebrity, like not being left alone when out to dinner, but asked if there weren't some perks to being well known.

"There are," said Hanks. "I've met two U.S. Presidents."

I turned to Dee and said, "Listen to this, Tom Hanks has met two U.S. Presidents and gets bothered by everyone when he's out to dinner. I've met four Presidents and nobody bothers me at dinner except our friends."

My first Presidential encounter was in the summer of 1987, just after I joined the board of the ABA. The association had, since the Hoover administration, given books to the White House Family Library with each new administration. President Reagan had been in office for six years, and a presentation date had finally been arranged during our national convention in D.C.

Our entourage arrived at the White House—twenty board members and staff—cleared security, and was ushered into the Roosevelt room just outside the Oval Office. We were met there by the smiling, jocular President. Though not a fan of his politics, I was charmed by his personality. ABA was about to publish an English edition of an encyclopedia that had first been published in Europe, and we brought the French edition for the presentation.

President Reagan looked at the tome and said, "I took French at Eureka College. A funny thing happened just after I graduated. I went to France with some friends. We were driving into a small village and wanted to get something to eat. I was the only one who spoke French. After rehearsing in my head what I would say, we spotted a gendarme. 'Bonjour,' I said. 'Bonjour,' said the gendarme. I repeated my carefully rehearsed question, asking where we might find a good place to eat. He pointed down the road, rapidly giving directions. 'Merci,' I said, and we drove off. One of my friends turned to me and asked what the gendarme had said. 'I don't have a clue,' I said."

I had two more opportunities to present books in the White House. The next was with President George H.W. Bush. Not only was the President in the Oval Office for the presentation, so was First Lady Barbara Bush.

After we had handed one particular book to the First Lady, she turned to the President.

"Have you read this book?" she asked. "You should really read this book."

Each of the booksellers in the room would gladly have had Barbara Bush recommending books in their stores with that same enthusiasm.

The presentation to President Clinton was the most satisfying. After some opening conversation the President asked, "Did you folks bring me some books?"

We acknowledged that we had.

"You know," he said. "Every Sunday when we come home from church I take a stack of books out onto the Truman porch and read for hours."

Sweeter words were never heard by a bookseller.

In early August that year I got a phone call.

"Chuck, I'd like you to go to Singapore." The voice on the other end of the line was that of my friend, fellow ABA board member and chair of the education committee Jerry Rehm.

"Jerry, I thought you were going. What happened?"

"My ex-wife is moving to New Mexico with the kids, and I have to make a decision about renewing my bookstore lease. I just can't go right now."

This was three weeks before the beginning of a booksellers school for the Singapore Booksellers Association that was to be taught by a member of the ABA Education Committee—until that point, Jerry.

"Will you go do this?" he asked.

"Let me talk to Dee," I said. I had little doubt that Dee would approve, especially if she were asked to go along, and I was right. Except for brief forays into Canada and Mexico and our trip to St. Martin, neither of us had done any foreign travel and we didn't have passports—none were needed in those days for the foreign destinations we had visited. Having been assured that we could get the documents expedited, we agreed to go.

I had heard that jet lag could be debilitating, especially on the third day after arrival—the day the booksellers school would begin. The store carried a book, *Overcoming Jet Lag* by Dr. Charles F. Ehret and Lynne Waller Scanlon (unfortunately, now out of print), but I had not had reason to peruse it. Now I did. The program had been developed for diplomats and involved some dietary changes—including caffeine usage—in the last few days before departure, as well as putting oneself on destination time on boarding the plane.

We left late at night and we weren't supposed to sleep until the plane departed Hawaii. It became clear that Singapore Airlines had fairly earned its reputation, as the flight attendants continued to bring us water—hydration is an important anti-jet lag component—and ask if we needed anything. We may have been the only passengers who were awake for that leg of the flight.

Rather than resting on arrival, we took our bags to our room at the Regional English Language Center and set out to visit Singapore's botanic garden. In the ninety degree heat, with equal humidity, we strolled around the central pond, examined a display of intricate bonsai, and gloried in the exotic tropical plants.

After our first introduction to Singapore's spicy cuisine, we strolled in and out of a series of high-rise shopping malls along Orchard Road and headed back to our room, fully exhausted. Neither of us had any trouble sleeping.

On Saturday morning we met Winston Yap for a tour of local bookstores. Two chains—MPH and Times—dominated the market, and very few independent stores existed. The stores were very clean, carefully organized, well-lighted, and extremely large at ten to twenty thousand square feet. This was two years before Barnes & Noble opened its first superstore. We had seen the future. We just didn't know it.

The bookstores were crowded with browsers, as were many of the other shops in the several malls we visited. Shopping, we soon learned, is a favorite pastime in Singapore. We were struck by the fact that most books were wrapped in plastic. A browser had to take the book to a clerk if he or she wanted to look inside.

When we stopped for coffee mid-afternoon, Winston was surprised that we were holding up so well, having just arrived the day before. "When we travel from the U.S., we're totally exhausted," he said. Dee explained the jet lag program. We had become—and remain—two of its greatest promoters.

On Sunday we explored more of the city on foot, and I spent some time in final preparation for the classes, which would begin the next morning. The Singapore Booksellers Association had asked ABA to provide a school for their booksellers similar to those taught in the U.S.

Monday morning I looked out upon a group of thirty eager

and anxious faces. Most of the students were from Singapore, but a few had come from Malaysia and other Southeast Asian countries. Quite a few worked for the chains, some came from University bookstores, and a few independents were in attendance as well.

"Mr. Robinson would like you to know that he would like you to ask questions and make comments throughout his presentation," Winston Yap said in his introduction. "And the students would like Mr. Robinson to know that they're not accustomed to doing that in this culture. So, we'll all do our best to make this work."

The students, as Winston had forewarned me, were very reluctant to interact during the sessions. Questions to the class that would elicit great chatter in schools back home were met with silence. Tea breaks, however, were a much different story. I was besieged with questions and comments, and the buzz of conversation in the room was electric.

The school continued for four full days, and on Friday I was the speaker at a special association luncheon. That evening I was the guest of honor at a dinner at a wonderful Hong Kong-style Chinese restaurant. During the meal another of the guests said, "I see you're enjoying the meal. Perhaps I shouldn't tell you what's in these dishes."

"I don't think you could dissuade me from eating this, no matter what's in it," I said.

"Are you part Singaporean?" he asked.

The guest of honor at a Chinese meal is often offered the eye of the fish. To avoid possible embarrassment with a western guest, the eye was offered to the retiring president of the Singapore Booksellers Association who, of course, ate it.

A few years later, while traveling with friends in Italy and having been served a whole fish, I told the story.

"You wouldn't have eaten the eye, would you?" said our friend Jan.

"Of course I would have."

"No you wouldn't," said Jan.

At that I plucked the eye from the fish and popped it in my mouth. Luckily for me the fish had been fried and the eyeball was totally desiccated. Our friend nearly fainted.

We spent a couple more days exploring Singapore, then three days in Hong Kong before returning to the U.S. The first international ABA booksellers school was over—other booksellers would teach several more in Singapore and Eastern Europe. And Dee and I had been bitten by the international travel bug.

During the years that the American Booksellers Association owned and operated the national trade show, the board was involved in choosing venues. Because the event drew nearly 50,000 people, the host city would reap considerable revenue and many cities were vying to land the show.

In the winter of 1988, Miami was courting the association at our winter board meeting. They picked us up at our hotel to whisk us off to one spot for drinks and on to another for dinner. Our entourage included twenty board members, some spouses, and ABA staff. To accommodate that group, the convention bureau had sent a fleet of white stretch limos.

As the limos arrived, it became evident that other folks in front of the hotel were wondering just who this group was that was traveling in such style. Kevin McCaffrey, a bookseller from New Orleans, was in our limo. Sensing an opportunity to have some fun with the curious crowd on the sidewalk, Kevin leaned out the door and, in his best British rocker imitation, yelled to an imagined aide, "And don't forget me fuckin' guitar." To this day I can't see a limo without thinking about Rockin' Kevin.

In 1983, law professor Catharine MacKinnon and feminist activist Andrea Dworkin wrote an antipornography ordinance for the city of Minneapolis. The law they proposed would have allowed victims of sexual attacks to sue producers and distributors of pornography if the attacker claimed that the material made him do it. The ordinance was twice-passed and twice-vetoed before the pair moved on to propose the same law in Indianapolis. There it was enacted but found unconstitutional in a 1985 case the American Booksellers Association brought against Mayor William H. Hudnut III.

A referendum on the same law was voted down in Cambridge, Massachusetts, in 1985. In 1988, an initiative was launched in Bellingham to put the ordinance on the ballot. City Attorney Bruce Disend advised the city council that the law was unconstitutional and recommended that it not be placed on the ballot. The council agreed and was sued by proponents of the measure. A judge opined that the measure was "not all that unconstitutional," causing both Disend and me to wonder if that was like "a little bit pregnant." The measure went on the November ballot and was passed.

Joined by the Washington State Library Association, the Pacific Northwest Booksellers Association, the American Booksellers Association, and three individual plaintiffs—artist Tom Sherwood, journalist and novelist Brenda Wilbee, and librarian Dana Johnson Verhey—we immediately sued the city of Bellingham. The city chose not to defend the ordinance, and the case was heard in federal court in Seattle the following February, with proponents of the measure intervening to defend the law.

In a question to Deborah Maranville, attorney for the intervenors, the judge noted that a similar ordinance had been found unconstitutional in Indianapolis, based on the overly broad definition of pornography. Maranville acknowledged that was the case.

"How have you changed that definition?" the judge asked.

"We have not, Your Honor," Maranville said.

Though the judge did not hand down her decision until

some weeks later, it seemed clear to many in the courtroom, from the look on the judge's face, how she would rule. On February 9, 1989, she ruled the ordinance unconstitutional.

Just over four years later, I appeared on a panel with Catharine MacKinnon. During the discussion I pointed out that bookstores could be sued for carrying material that a criminal claimed had caused him to commit a sexual attack. Ms. MacKinnon said, "That's a lie." It wasn't until after the panel that I was able to confront her and point out the part of the law that proved my point. "Oh, you're talking about the trafficking provision," she said. Of course I was talking about the trafficking provision. We would have been defined as a trafficker.

In the two and a half years following our expansion and the addition of the Colophon Café we kept packing more and more books into the store and, fortunately, selling more and more out the door. It had also become difficult to get a spot for lunch at the Colophon.

We sat down in the café one day to talk with our landlord, Ken Imus, and his son Brad. We were interested in expanding the bookstore and café into the area below our present space. It was a dirty, undeveloped space that, in recent years, had only been used for storage and a Halloween haunted house. It would take a lot of work.

"Well, let's go down and take a look," said Ken.

After downing our coffee we trudged around the building to the back garage-door entry—the stairway had been boarded over and now served as a closet in the bookstore. Our eyes were greeted by rock walls, brick pillars, and huge timber beams. Ken, who had been somewhat skeptical, now became animated. One of the things I've always loved about Ken is his vision. He's a very visual person who "sees" the way things might be. It didn't take long for his vision to overcome his skepticism.

"Let's do it," he said.

And that was that. Soon work began in the basement area as we prepared for a mid-June opening of the expanded café and bookstore. Our Spring 1988 edition of our newsletter—then called *The Village Voice*—said this about the impending opening:

"Most of you know how crowded it was in the store during the Fall season and how little room there seems to be on any shelf. The new space should alleviate those problems. There will also be more room for readings which are, by the way, becoming quite packed. The children's book section will grow by leaps and bounds, and many other sections will at least double. Most of all, we hope to restore the feeling of leisurely browsing that existed when we first opened, including chairs and just a bit more elbow room."

We had learned, with our first move, and nearly every adjustment that we had made in the store, that people are very anxious about change. A portion of the article in that newsletter attempted to address those fears, promising nooks and crannies—just as the current space had—and Fairhaven-like touches of leaded glass and an old phone booth. It also tried to assure folks that the Colophon Café would be able to give them "more of what you've come to love." That included additional seating and an expanded kitchen that would allow menu options including "the salads you've been asking for."

Brad Imus, Ken's son, built a large rectangular box on the main level of the store, over the area where the stairway was cut through. At our request he cut some small holes in the box—the type one sees in the walls around new building construction in large cities—so folks could spy on what was happening. The fact that one could not see much through the holes didn't deter folks from peeking. The excitement about the expansion was palpable. Everyone wanted to know what it would look like and when it would open.

On June 13, 1988, the box was ripped apart and the store

nearly doubled in size. The Colophon became more than twice its original size, finally had a real kitchen, and gained additional outdoor seating on the cobblestones behind the building. Once again we felt like we had breathing room.

That expansion required the largest addition to our staff that we've ever made at one time—seven people, almost a 60% increase. To be certain that we would have the group well-trained before opening, we brought them on board about five weeks early. Our first training meeting took place on May 5, 1988, appropriately in the lower level of Dos Padres Restaurant. That group has been forever known as the Cinco de Mayo Seven, and four of the seven remained attached to the business for a long time.

Paul Haskins had just turned twenty-one when he came to the store for an interview as we were hiring for the expansion and were talking to candidates in our low-ceilinged loft office. Paul, who hadn't seen the low side of six feet for a few years, ducked as he entered the office. "You have to be able to stand up in this office to be hired here," I joked. "I'll cut off my legs," he said, without hesitation. We hired him. He began working that spring and was with us for seventeen and a half years, working as a bookseller, book buyer, receiver, and our chief technology expert. He was also part of a team that helped plan the new building.

Dave Lippiatt, another of the May 5th cohort, remained at the store for seven years. Then, after some time away to work at the brand new Boundary Bay Brewery, ride his bike across the country, teach English in Japan, and work in a couple of other bookstores, he came and left over the course of the next several years, returning most recently in the fall of 2008.

Stephanie Howard was a sophomore at Western when she joined as part of that group. She continued with us as our children's book buyer for a couple of years after she finished graduate school, before marrying and moving to Seattle where she became the children's book buyer for UW's bookstore, then the Northwest sales representative for Scholastic Publishing

Company. She took a hiatus while her kids were very young but, in the past couple of years, she's once again been working part time in a bookstore.

A fourth member of the group, Pam Helberg, left Village Books to open her own bookstore in Seattle, Fremont Place Books. The store, under new ownership, is still in operation. Pam rejoined us for a brief time after selling her store and returning to Bellingham, then left to work in the computer business.

Two other long-term folks became part of the staff that summer. Jim Spiedel joined us on his birthday, July 21. He had been a teacher and then owned his own bookstore in Santa Fe before moving to Bellingham. He took over remainder buying shortly after coming to the store, and helped launch our used book program a few years later. He continues to buy the bargain books one sees around the store and heads up the used book department, training new buyers as needed and keeping everything running smoothly.

Alaine Borgias came to work on that same day with Jim. She and Paul Haskins took a liking to one another, but hadn't quite connected before she left on a European adventure a little over a year later. On her return to Bellingham, Alaine took a job elsewhere as an office manager, but she and Paul renewed their acquaintance. In the summer of 1992, when I became president of ABA and shortly after the birth of their son Finnian, Alaine came back to the store to take on a number of marketing tasks. Over the next thirteen years she built our author program to about two hundred fifty events per year, oversaw our advertising, and helped grow our *Chuckanut Reader* from a thirty-two page to a forty-eight page publication. She and Paul left the store in 2005 and now publish *NW Adventures Magazine*.

By the late '80s, managing our burgeoning author-event program was becoming another sort of adventure. While we have occasionally become anxious about whether an author might show up, we're nearly always nervous about whether anyone will show up to see the author. It doesn't help that Bellingham is such a last-minute community. At five minutes until seven the Readings Gallery might be empty as our stomachs are turning flip flops, only to fill up nicely by the time the author is introduced—or, sometimes, after that. We've only had a very few occasions when no one showed up. Fortunately, authors are generally understanding and are nice folks to talk with.

The size of the audience can also be much smaller than expected, a disappointment to both the store and the author. In the late '80s Krista Hunter was managing our reading series, which included some very notable authors—W.P. Kinsella, Ivan Doig, and Tom Bodett among them. After one particularly disappointing turnout, Krista asked me what I thought we should do.

"Give Rick Simonson at Elliott Bay a call," I said. Rick had already been generous in pointing authors and publishers our way, and he ran one of the best author programs in the country. I figured he'd have some good advice for us. Krista explained the situation to Rick, lamenting the poor attendance, and asked his advice.

"Do more events," Rick said.

Thinking that perhaps he didn't quite understand the situation, she said, "But folks aren't coming to the ones we're holding. Why would we do more?"

"People need to think of you when they think of author events," Rick said. "You don't want folks to ask *if* you're holding an event a particular evening, you want them to call the store and ask what the event *is* that evening. You want to become known for events."

That was, undoubtedly, one of the single best pieces of advice we've ever received. We began gearing up the program, and within a very short time were holding a dozen or more author events each month and continuing to grow.

On February 14, 1989, following the September, 1988, publication of *The Satanic Verses*, a fatwa was issued by the Ayatollah Ruhollah Komeini calling for the assassination of its author Salman Rushdie. Near chaos ensued in the book world, and Rushdie went into hiding. Threats were issued against his publisher, bookstores were firebombed in the U.K. and U.S.—including our friends at Cody's in Berkeley—and national bookstore chains announced they wouldn't carry the book, prompting a satirical skit on "Saturday Night Live." Village Books, along with hundreds of other independent bookstores, openly displayed and sold *The Satanic Verses.*

The American Booksellers Association had to make special arrangements for our national convention in Washington, D.C. We hired the same security company that one of the television networks had used for the Olympics in Seoul the year before: ex-spooks in four-hundred-dollar suits with sunglasses and single earphones. They came with bomb-sniffing dogs who scoured the entire convention center each morning before the opening, and they manned airport-like metal detectors through which attendees passed on entering.

Fortunately, there were no incidents at the convention except for a few protests from booksellers about the security, and especially about the fact that there were VIPs with special pins— myself included—who were exempted from the screenings. We all breathed a deep sigh of relief when the convention ended.

One afternoon a month or so later, a Middle Eastern gentleman walked into Village Books carrying a small styrofoam cooler. He asked if he could leave it at the counter while he browsed. Thinking nothing of it, Norman said, "Sure," and set the cooler behind the counter as the gentleman strolled into the fiction section. After some time passed, Norman looked around, could no longer see the man in the store, and suddenly had a feeling of anxiety. Just as he was ready to grab the cooler and get it out of the store, the gentleman came back to the counter, thanked

Norman for keeping it, and quietly strolled out the door. In retrospect it was funny, but at the time, we realized how the fatwa and subsequent incidents had permeated our consciousness.

The unexpected sometimes happens at author events. Shortly after expanding into the lower level of the building, we experimented with broadcasting events throughout the store. On one of her visits, Ann Rule was talking about a time in her career when she was writing romance stories. She was explaining where she got some of her plot ideas.

"I was looking for a very unusual medical condition that I could use in a story," she said, "so I asked my gynecologist if he could think of any rare birth defect that might figure into a story. He said that sometimes girls are born without a vagina."

Ann quickly turned to me and said, "Chuck, I hope this isn't going out through the whole store."

I just smiled and nodded.

At another event, not long after Ann's, Jonathan Raban was taking questions from the audience when one of the attendees asked, "Don't you think that the English use language better than Americans?"

Jonathan, English himself, said, "No, I actually believe Americans are much more inventive in their use of language. The English are quite staid."

"But don't you think the English have a better education system?" the questioner persisted.

"There are big problems with the education systems in both countries," Rabin said. "I wouldn't say the English system is better."

After taking questions from elsewhere in the room, he saw that the earlier questioner had his hand raised once again. Raban looked at him and said, "No, I tried with you twice."

Looking around the room, I saw no other hands raised, so

I tried to break the tension by asking, "What are you working on now?"

"I never talk about what I'm working on," he said. "I think it's bad luck."

It was clear that it was time to thank Jonathan and move on to the book signing.

"I've never been anyplace where people knew my poetry so well."

Those were the words of Wendell Berry as we drove him to Seattle after his December 1988 appearance at the store. On an extremely rare tour, he had come to talk about and read from his new novel *Remembering*. When he finished, he asked the audience if he might read a poem or two. They were thrilled. So thrilled that, when he finished those poems, they began requesting others—some by page number in particular collections. Warm smiles of pleasure adorned the faces of the audience as they sat in rapt attention, listening to the melodic midwestern voice recite their favorite lines. No one would have objected if he had continued for hours. I suspect that even he would have loved to go on longer, but knew there was still a long drive ahead.

Some authors were not well-known when they first came to the store, but soared to fame later. A prime example is David Guterson. His family outnumbered others in the Readings Gallery when he read from his first book of short stories, *The Country Ahead of Us, The Country Behind*. He packed the place when he later came for *Snow Falling on Cedars*.

As the '80s came to a close, we were beginning to feel comfortable in our larger quarters, author events had become a major part of our store's identity, and we were ready to launch into a new decade with a great crew of booksellers. But, once again, unexpected change loomed on the horizon.

Chapter 4

A Taste for Travel

By the time the new '90s decade dawned, we were beginning to feel comfortable in the expanded space we had created two years earlier. Our staffing was stable and the business was doing fairly well. Though there was still plenty of work to do, we were beginning to feel the need for a real break.

Since returning from Singapore, Dee and I hadn't travelled outside U.S. borders. When I joined the ABA board, Gail See, the ABA's immediate past president, had offered advice. "Chuck, when you travel for ABA meetings or conventions take some extra time, even if it's just a day," she said. "I've just flown in and out of so many places over the past few years. I so regret not having seen what was there."

I took Gail at her word and have tried to schedule an extra day or two, sometimes longer, with meetings I've attended. One meeting in Miami got us to the Keys, and another to see a nephew in Orlando. From a booksellers school in St. Petersburg, Florida, we saw Sanibel and Captiva Islands and the Ringling Museums. Boston meetings afforded us visits to Cape Cod and Martha's Vineyard. We traveled by train to a Chicago convention and visited family nearby, as well as friends in Denver on the return trip, and the many occasions we've had to be in New York have allowed us to see much of what the Big Apple has to offer.

We were now in our forties and thought, mistakenly, that we must be the only people of that age not to have traveled to Europe. Many of our vintage had backpacked the continent after college, while we had begun teaching and then moved on to bookselling. Europe had passed us by, or vice versa.

So we pulled out our maps, went to a Rick Steves travel seminar, and began planning a serious European trip. Thinking that this might be our only European adventure, we tried to pack everything into one grand tour. Finally realizing that we didn't want to have an "if it's Tuesday it must be Belgium" experience, we began whittling it down.

"I think we're going to have to cut out Spain," Dee said.

"You're right, and I think Rome will have to go, too," I said. "Let's just go as far south as Florence."

In spite of our trimming, there were some places we were determined to see. We had a friend living in Prague who insisted we must see the city before there were Coke signs hanging everywhere. For years we had longed to see Paris, and we weren't about to flit in and out of the City of Light. We settled on six weeks.

On Labor Day, 1991, we lifted off from Bellingham International Airport. Before leaving we had made arrangements to call early each Saturday morning, which was just before closing on Friday evening back home. The staff was asked to route all questions and concerns to Mitchell so we would talk to him and answer questions, lend advice, and make important decisions from a distance. Each week the conversation went something like this:

"Hi, Mitchell, it's Chuck."

"Hi, Chuck, where are you?"

"We're in (*fill in the blank*). How are things there?"

"They're fine."

"Any problems?"

"None that I know of," Mitchell said. "How's your weather?"

"Fine, how's yours?"

"It's been raining," he said.

And so it went for six weeks. When we returned, several nearly-forgotten projects had been completed, the store looked great, and sales had increased in our absence. We joked that we should have just stayed away and had checks sent.

Paris was our first destination. We had arranged to travel together for the first two weeks with friends from the Midwest who would meet up with us after their travels in Switzerland. The night they came into Paris, we ate dinner at Cremerie Restaurant Polidor.

Seated in typical European style, across from one another at a long table, we were catching up on each others' lives. A young couple sat to my right, facing each other across the table and conversing in French.

"How are your kids?" Dee asked our friends.

"They're not really kids anymore, but they're fine," Jan said.

"How do you like Bellingham and how's the bookstore?" John asked.

"Excuse me," said the young man across the table, this time in English. "Do you own Village Books in Bellingham?"

I was stunned. On another continent, thousands of miles from home, and this guy is asking me about our bookstore?

"Uh, yes we do," I said.

"We love your store," the young woman said.

"How do you know our store?"

The couple explained that they lived in Paris and worked at the Abbey Bookshop, which was owned by Canadian bookseller Brian Spence.

"We used to live in Vancouver and came to Bellingham a lot," said the young man. "We always visited Village Books."

We took the train from Paris to Strasbourg to pick up the leased car we would use for the rest of our journey. The brand new car was waiting for us at a Peugeot dealership. We were told that we would have to stop for fuel soon, and a short distance away we stopped to fill up, but we couldn't find the release for the gas tank cover. Even our friend John, an accomplished mechanic who had rebuilt several cars, was of no help. I turned to the man at the next pump.

"Parlez-vous anglais?"

"That's all I speak," he said.

That was a good thing, as I had nearly exhausted my French. In spite of our being able to communicate, he couldn't help us. Nor could the attendant inside the station who may, or may not, have understood what I was asking.

Finally, through a series of trial and error machinations, we learned that the ignition key had to be turned to a particular point before the cover would pop open. With the tank full, we were on our way.

That was the only trouble we had with the car. We were even able to communicate with the Italian garage attendant in Lucca well enough to have the car's first oil change taken care of. While we love train travel, especially in dependable Europe, the car allowed us to be on our own schedule and get to places we otherwise would not have seen.

That first trip to Europe took us through parts of France, Germany, Austria, Italy, Switzerland, Lichtenstein, and Czecho-slovakia. Our friends were with us from Paris through Germany, including visits to Rothenburg ob der Tauber and Dachau, and down through Austria to Italy, where we went to Venice and Cinque Terre before they flew home.

The logical itinerary would have been for us to go from Rothenburg to Prague, but in spite of some coaxing from us, our friends weren't interested in going there. So after they left us in Italy, we toured Florence, southern France, and Switzerland before heading across Austria to Vienna on our way to Prague.

Our visit to Mozart's birth house in Salzburg was especial-ly magical. Any tour through the home of the musical genius would have been special, but we were fortunate to enter behind a group of folks on a U.S. university music tour.

One room displayed several instruments—his childhood violin, a clavichord, and the pianoforte on which he composed much of his music. Normally the tour group would have moved on to the next room after viewing the instruments. This time, however, the docent sat down at the pianoforte, opened the cover with a small key, and began to play. We were hearing notes from the same instrument on which Mozart had composed many of his symphonies between 1771 and 1781. I can never hear a Mozart piece without thinking about that wonderful experience.

Because we were traveling in typical Rick Steves style, we rolled into Vienna on a Friday evening in early October without hotel reservations. It hadn't crossed our minds that the entire city, as well as all of Austria, was commemorating the 200th year since Mozart's death. We couldn't find a room in our budget range anywhere. Finally, standing at the front desk of yet another full hotel, we abandoned our budget and asked if they could call and find us a room at any price. Still nothing.

We got back in our car, thinking that by driving a few miles out of town we'd certainly find a vacancy. The ring road was made more confusing by construction detours and signs we didn't fully understand. In the midst of our third loop around the city, we were likely looking as much for the sign of a marriage counselor or divorce lawyer as we were the correct exit.

Finally finding the exit we were looking for, we headed south and began stopping at each interchange on the Autostrasse, inquiring about a room. No luck. No luck. No luck. Finally, frustrated and tired, we pulled into a rest area, reclined the seats, pulled our coats around us and tried to sleep.

Neither of us is certain just how much sleep we got that night. After dark the temperature had dropped quickly, and we would shiver ourselves awake, start the car to warm up, and begin the cycle once again. Very early the next morning we drove back to Vienna and went directly to the visitor housing office.

While the room we got was the worst of our entire trip, it sure beat sleeping in the car.

We left Vienna and drove across then-undivided Czechoslovakia to Prague. The placid, pastoral drive was mostly uneventful, except for one rest stop. Though we expected something more primitive than U.S. Interstate restrooms, we were totally unprepared for what we encountered. I nearly gagged when I walked in, but, holding my breath, was able to quickly relieve myself and leave. Dee returned to the car having witnessed, in her words, "The filthiest toilet I have ever seen." She decided she could wait.

We had met John Allison when he worked for ABA's trade magazine. He had moved to Prague to teach English and work for the English language newspaper *Prognosis*. Soon after he arrived he was hired as an advisor to the Mayor of Prague, and through attrition became the Senior American Advisor to the Mayor. After leaving the Mayor's office, John served as an advisor to President Vaclac Havel before returning to the U.S. All of this without speaking a word of Czech.

John had made friends with a man named Victor Faktor, a former government surveyor who was also a writer and publisher. Victor and his family had a very comfortable bedroom and bathroom, with a separate entrance, in their home in a neighborhood near Prague Castle. Because U.S. dollars were highly favored over Czech currency, Victor rented the room to us for twenty dollars per night.

While the accommodation was likely the best dollar value we had on our entire trip, the price was not the best part of it. The Faktors gave us a real insider's view of Prague. Victor took us to a poetry reading at a small bookstore where they served newly made wine, and some of the Faktor's friends, including

John Allison and his girlfriend, joined us at their local pub, a place no tourist would ever have found.

As we wound through the soccer stadium, we wondered if this might be a joke played on unsuspecting guests. We arrived at a plain door, which could well have been the locker room. It wasn't. When the door opened we were met with laughter and chatter and the smell of beer. It was, indeed, their local pub, and it was the smokiest room I had ever witnessed.

We drank beer, ate dinner, and finished off with a couple of glasses of Becherovka, an herbal liqueur made with anise seed, cinnamon, and more than thirty other herbs. Its alcohol content is 38%. When the bill arrived, I tried to pay it, but our hosts wouldn't hear of it. The total for the entire evening, for nine of us, was about $12.

We spent four nights in Prague and loved every moment. We've heard that the city has become much more expensive and has developed a much more Western atmosphere, but we would love to go back. Unlike many European cities, Prague was never bombed, so it still has its old buildings.

I mentioned to Victor how beautiful I thought the city was. "It's because we had Italian architects," he said.

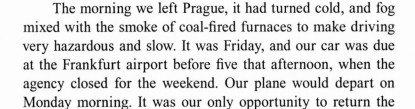

The morning we left Prague, it had turned cold, and fog mixed with the smoke of coal-fired furnaces to make driving very hazardous and slow. It was Friday, and our car was due at the Frankfurt airport before five that afternoon, when the agency closed for the weekend. Our plane would depart on Monday morning. It was our only opportunity to return the car, or own it.

As if the fog weren't enough to worry about, there was a long line at the Czech/German border, followed by a major accident that slowed traffic to a crawl on the Autobahn. We were getting nervous. An hour out of Frankfurt, we called the agency to assure them we were on our way, and we arrived at the office with minutes to spare.

We had chosen Frankfurt as our final destination for two reasons. It was the closest city to Prague where we could return the car, and the Frankfurter Buchmesse (Frankfurt Book Fair), the largest and best-known book fair in the world, was in session at Messe Frankfurt, an exhibition grounds used exclusively for large trade shows and congresses.

The ABA was sharing a booth, and several members of the staff were attending. Because Frankfurt hotels charge premium prices during the fairs, the ABA folks were staying a half hour train ride north in the village of Butzbach and had booked a room for us as well.

The 1991 ABA convention in New York occupied much of Javits Convention Center, but the Frankfurt Book Fair dwarfed it. Building after building was filled with books. One entire structure displayed nothing but coffee table-style art books, and another pavilion was just for German books. The first three days of the fair were open to just the book trade, with the public being welcomed the last two days. Wandering through the thousands of books was a thrill, even though we could read only a fraction of them. Nearly as exciting was talking with our friends and catching up on news from home.

During the previous six weeks we only occasionally saw English language newspapers and, when we did, it was often the *International Herald Tribune*. We loved the *Tribune* with its distinctive European slant, and we seldom missed the ethnocentric reporting we were accustomed to back home. But now, as we were preparing to return Stateside, we were anxious to learn what was happening there.

The Clarence Thomas Supreme Court confirmation hearings began less than two weeks after we left for Europe and had not yet concluded when we were in Butzbach with our ABA friends. We didn't know where things stood. The wife of one of the staff members had come to Germany with him, and she eagerly filled us in on the hearings, which she had followed carefully before leaving home. The 52-48 vote confirming his nomination was announced over the intercom in our airplane just as we touched down in Chicago.

It was with that first European trip that Rick Steves became our travel guru. One thing we had learned about was traveling light. Rick loves asking folks if, when returning from a vacation, they wished they had taken more with them. We still marvel, as we're stuffing the car for a couple of days in Seattle or Portland, that we lived for six weeks out of a bag that fit under an airline seat.

Rick's books were also our guiding lights. We had thoroughly studied *Europe Through the Back Door* and his books on history and art, as well as the *Europe in 21 Days* book that was so popular at the time (Rick has since published numerous country and city guides, and combined his art and history books).

We learned quickly that we weren't the only Americans who relied on Rick. We saw the guides everywhere. As we were waiting in line at the train station in La Spezia, getting tickets to Cinque Terre, we noted that four of the five people in the line had one of his books in hand.

One tip that was tough for a bookseller, or any book lover, was to tear the travel guide into sections and discard the sections as one moved on to the next destination. However, we steeled ourselves and, before we left for Europe, tore the guide into sections, leaving behind those parts for places we wouldn't be seeing. It may not have saved a lot of weight, but as we added small souvenirs we were leaving something else behind. As with backpackers who cut the handles off of toothbrushes, every little bit counts.

The trip to Europe proved to be the calm before the storm. When Book Shop Santa Cruz was shaken to the ground in the 1989 Loma Prieta earthquake, its owner Neal Coonerty had to step aside from being ABA president. Joyce Meskis accepted the presidency, and I the vice presidency of the association.

Corporate big box stores had begun to open, and illegal trade practices were suspected. Joyce and I were at the helm, and the perfect storm was about to hit.

Chapter 5

The Eye of the Storm 1990–1994

While booksellers, librarians, and avid readers are ever-hopeful that we have, finally, put an end to censorship, our more realistic nature tells us that's not the case. In the spring of 1990 we were reminded, right here in Bellingham, of that truth.

Feminist activist Nikki Craft destroyed four copies of *Esquire* magazine in our store. She had come in with a friend and spotted the magazine, which was themed "The Secret Life of the American Wife." One of the features in the issue was entitled "Your Wife: An Owner's Manual." Interestingly, an offended staff member had posted a note beside the magazine (an action we encouraged) that said, "This is sick, sexist trash."

Also offended by the issue, Ms. Craft carried the four copies of the magazine to the counter and said, "What would you do if someone tore these up?"

The staff person, relatively new to the store, attempted some humor. "I guess I'd have to call the Green Berets." Ms. Craft was not amused, and tore up the magazines.

Dee and I had left the store shortly before the incident, and received a call asking what should be done. I said, "Call the police."

Knowing the police were coming, Ms. Craft waited for some time for them to arrive. Finally losing patience, she gave her name and the address where she was staying, and left the store. When the officer arrived at her address and attempted to present a citation, Ms. Craft refused to accept it, insisting on being arrested.

Once in jail, she refused to post bond and remained there for 22 nights. Released on her own recognizance to speak at a conference at WWU, she was not readmitted to the jail. The court later ordered her to pay $11 for the magazines.

The incident prompted much discussion in the community. In the midst of the controversy, I wrote the following as a guest columnist in *The Bellingham Herald*:

Protesters would impose censorship

Events of the past few weeks have again brought issues of censorship to the fore in Bellingham. On May 23, nationally-known feminist activist Nikki Craft entered Village Books and destroyed four copies of the June issue of *Esquire* magazine in a protest of its "sexist articles." She was arrested and jailed on a charge of malicious mischief.

A group led by Lucy Colvin arrived at the store the next day with KIRO television news personnel in tow, asking us to return the issue to the publisher in protest of its content and to drop the charges against Nikki Craft. We refused.

The actions of Craft, Colvin, the group with her that day, and subsequent picketers at the store bear out our ongoing contention that this is an issue of censorship, an attempt to block ideas from being expressed.

The proponents of Craft's actions say they don't want us to sell "sexist" literature. Do they really mean that or do they mean sexist literature with which they disagree? Do they really want us to cease selling the work of Andrea Dworkin and others whose ideas are very anti-male, thus sexist? Yes, just as there are black and Hispanic racists, there are feminist sexists.

Ideas are precious—whether we agree with them or not—and they are accorded a special status by our Constitution and are the basis of a democratic society. Craft's defenders hope that when faced with 20, 100, or 1,000 people who object to this "sexist" literature, we would withdraw it from sale. Do they also hope that if faced with that kind of pressure we would cease selling other types of material we carry—feminist, leftist, communist, Baptist?

There seems to be an underlying belief that if one bans an idea the ills of society that are in any way associated with that idea will miraculously disappear. Senator Joe McCarthy believed that. We don't.

The absence of pornography in Ireland and Muslim countries has not ended violence against women. As much as any of us may not like what they say, the speech of sexists (female or male) is, and should be, protected.

Craft's actions have been defended as acts of civil disobedience. As an advocate of civil disobedience, I would suggest that these defenders go back to the sources on the subject. I don't remember Thoreau, Gandhi, or King ever begging to have charges dropped. Nor did any of them recommend acts of civil disobedience as the first action to be taken. Furthermore, they suggest civil disobedience as acts of moral conscience, not media ploys.

I admire the dedication of Craft, Colvin, and others in bringing attention to gender power imbalance, stereotyping of genders, and violence against women. I also admire the organizing of this effort that brought media attention and even spurred me to write this.

But let's not fool ourselves that Craft has been wronged by being charged for an illegal action. She knew the consequences and she took the action. She, no doubt, hopes the cost is worth it. So do we.

When facing critical issues we all at times hope for a panacea, a quick fix, a magic cure. Censorship, like most supposed quick fixes, is not the answer. When one idea is censored, no idea is safe.

So if we don't censor ideas we don't like, what should we do? While I won't pretend to have an all-encompassing answer to these problems, I will suggest some starting points:

- Encourage publication of material that presents other views of women (there are many).
- Write letters to the editor of publications that publish articles that reinforce stereotypes and tell them what you think is wrong with their ideas.
- Suggest alternative ways of thinking.
- Challenge what others say about women.
- Work to encourage strong enforcement of legislation against rape and abuse and help others recognize those as crimes of violence, not the result of seduction.

I don't mean to suggest that the defenders of Craft have not done these things. I know many of them have and I know that the pace of progress has been frustrating.

We will all continue to face numerous attempts at censorship including, perhaps, a statewide initiative this fall. It would be easy to go for the magic cure. But let's attack the actions, not the ideas.

And keep in mind that it takes no courage to defend only those ideas with which you agree. You must defend those which you may find distasteful as well.

Many have spoken and written about this point, but perhaps Garrison Keillor explained it as well as anyone when he recently said, "I'm a Puritan myself and I see a great deal every day that is deeply offensive to me, but like most Americans I oppose censorship and suppression. It's wrong and it never works."

The next week in a publication called *The Fishwrapper*, Ms.

Craft in an open letter took me to task on several points of my guest column, including my implication that she had "begged" to have charges dropped. She ended her letter with, "Death to the Patriarchy." In the same issue my response appeared.

Dear Nikki Craft,

You point out, quite correctly, that I misled readers by implying that you begged to have charges dropped. You are, however, incorrect in asserting that it was only one of your supporters who entreated, beseeched, implored, yes, begged (1. to ask for as a gift, as charity, or a favor) us to drop charges against you and to quit carrying that issue of *Esquire*. We had about half-a-dozen phone calls that same morning from your supporters (before any notices of your arrest appeared in the media—imagine that) and Lucy Colvin showed up with a dozen or more folks, many of whom pleaded (dare I use the word?) your case.

Your contention that your "free speech" would have been maintained by having charges dropped is absurd. Few folks freely walking the streets of Bellingham over the past several weeks have garnered more press quotes (read "free speech") than you. You may, of course, offer that as proof of the efficacy of your actions. But, please don't argue at the same time that it would have been better to drop the charges. The quotes in Sunday's *Dallas Morning News* suggest that you were not altogether happy to be released. You also never address the point of why you think your illegal actions should not be prosecuted.

As for your arguments on civil disobedience, while you seem to "misrepresent and trivialize the messenger(s):" (Thoreau, Gandhi, and King) there was nothing in my argument that trivialized you. And for me to have misrepresented you would mean that what you did was not a "media ploy." Your own justifications defend your "tactics" as ones of which you feel your inspirers would approve.

Though I also respect the work of Goldman, Anthony, Malcolm X, and Hoffman (sometimes, but not always, from my armchair), I am surprised that you didn't also list Carry Nation, Rev. Donald Wildmon, Jesse Helms, and Phyllis Schlaffley—people who also have decided what it is that causes us to do the evil things we do and who are so ready to prevent us from having contact with those materials that "cause" the evil.

It would be senseless for me to deny being a liberal white boy First Amendment Fundamentalist. I came by some of it genetically and some by choice. I haven't met your straw men amongst my fellow L.W.B.F.A.F.'s who scream for the silencing of women. One could hardly be a First Amendment Fundamentalist ("someone who puts the First Amendment above all"—your definition in one of our phone conversations) and oppose the free speech of someone else.

Finally, you are, no doubt, correct that "the owner" (I'll assume this refers to me in this case and not my female partner) should spend more time browsing in our store's women's section. We could all stand to learn more about all of the crucial issues with which we are faced. I should tell you that I have browsed enough there to know that you do not speak for all feminists. Nancy Boreano, the publisher of Firebrand Books, while not a white boy, certainly fits your definition of a First Amendment Fundamentalist. The women at Seal Press do not support censorship tactics though they are as concerned as you (and I, though you may not believe it) about the imbalance of images of women being published. Betty Friedan certainly voiced opposition to your actions and others like them when she said, "To introduce censorship in the United States in the guise of suppressing pornography is extremely dangerous to women." So, while it may be easy to dismiss us liberal white boys as part of the patriarchy, it would be incredibly preposterous to dismiss these, and other, outspoken feminists who disagree with you. Don't belittle the fight against violence against women by dismissing the other women who raise their voices in speech that differs from yours. But there I go being paternalistic again.

Death to the Patriarchy... and all other forms of tyranny.

Writing about censorship in *The Washington Post*, Charles Trueheart noted the *Esquire* event and quoted me as saying, "If suppressing objectionable material amounts to 'civil disobedience,' as Craft has claimed, Mr. Thoreau, Mr. Gandhi, and Dr. King ... are rolling over in their graves."

Censorship issues were by no means confined to our corner of the world. The ABA, which had, throughout its ninety-year history, engaged in fights against censorship, formed a new organization in 1990—The American Booksellers Foundation for Free Expression (ABFFE)—to be able to more quickly and more effectively respond to censorship challenges. As vice president of the ABA at the time, I also served a two-year term as ABFFE's founding vice president, then returned to its board in 1996, where I served for the next ten years.

The launch of ABFFE was announced at a news conference at the 1990 ABA convention in Las Vegas that June. Judy Blume joined board members on the dais as the press was told that ABFFE would be "the bookseller's voice in the fight against censorship," and that our mission would be "to promote and protect the free exchange of ideas, particularly those contained in books, by opposing restrictions on the freedom of speech; issuing statements on significant free expression controversies; participating in legal cases involving First Amendment rights; collaborating with other groups with an interest in free speech; and providing education about the importance of free expression to booksellers, other members of the book industry, politicians, the press, and the public."

Twenty years later, ABFFE continues to be ever-vigilant and constantly active in censorship and privacy issues in every state in the nation. The organization's contribution to education that is most visible to the public is Banned Books Week, which ABFFE cosponsors with the American Library Association and other groups. And hardly a month goes by in which it is not engaged in legal battles in one state or another.

As the '80s waned, author events shifted mostly from signings to readings and talks. There were, however, a few authors who preferred to just sign books and could draw large crowds. Two writers in the early '90s drew huge crowds to signings at Village Books.

In June of 1990, famed bird book author Roger Tory Peterson came to the store to sign his new *Western Birds*. We set him at a table in the lower level of the store, near the door leading onto the cobblestones—this was before the Fairhaven Village Green was built. His wife, who had created the maps for the book, was seated next to him.

Long before the Petersons arrived that day, bird lovers had flocked to the store. A long line snaked out the door and along the cobblestones. Many well-loved copies of Peterson's past books were presented for an autograph, including a worn copy of a 1934 first edition of his *Field Guide to Birds*.

The next month Peterson was nearly drowned in a boating mishap in Maine. Fortunately, he was rescued and lived another six years before dying at his home a month before his eighty-eighth birthday.

Children's book author and illustrator Chris Van Allsburg, popular for his books *Jumanji* and *The Polar Express*, drew a crowd equal to Peterson's. But, because it was November—not

June—we had to keep the line inside of the store. We put Van Allsburg's table in the far corner of the lower level and wound the line across the room and up the stairs. Scores of young readers, parents, and teachers waited—most patiently—for the soft-spoken, bearded and bespectacled artist to sign their books.

When Bret Easton Ellis' *American Psycho* was published in 1991, we ordered just one copy, believing we had little market for the book. Then it met with protests all across the country. Tammy Bruce, national board member and president of the L.A. chapter of the National Organization for Women (NOW), led a boycott against the publisher, Knopf. Bellingham was not spared. Protesters appeared in front of Waldenbooks at Bellis Fair mall and on the sidewalk in front of Village Books to loudly read graphic excerpts from the book. We were also asked to stop carrying the book.

This, like many attempts at censorship, had the opposite effect the protesters desired. The only complaints we heard were about the protest itself. One came from a mother who was disturbed that her children had to hear the graphic, violently sexual language. Sales of the book increased dramatically with the attention the protests received, including a big story at the top of the local section in the *Herald*. One customer told us, as she bought the book, that she had no intention of reading it. "I just don't want people telling me what I can and can't read," she said.

By the beginning of the new decade, several large independent bookstores had been created, among them The Tattered Cover in Denver, Books & Company in Dayton, Oxford Books in Atlanta, and Borders Books in Ann Arbor. Yes, you read that correctly—Borders Books was an independent bookstore, begun by brothers Tom and Louis Borders and expanded into a very large space in 1980.

The chain stores, Waldenbooks (owned at that time by K-Mart) and B. Dalton (owned by Barnes & Noble), existed primarily in malls, and it wasn't until September of 1990 that Barnes & Noble opened its first "superstore" in Roseville, Minnesota, followed shortly by one in suburban Detroit. A new era had dawned, and though we would not face a large chain store in Bellingham for another five years, the entire bookselling business was being thrown into turmoil.

In June of 1992 I became president of ABA, and nearly half of my time each day was devoted to association work. As the spokesperson for the organization, each day I would receive phone calls from reporters asking about issues facing bookstores and publishers—most revolving around big box stores. Some calls were from small, hometown newspapers. Others were from *USA Today, The New York Times,* or *The Wall Street Journal.*

I soon learned that there were basically two kinds of reporters. The first was the investigative journalist who wanted to get to the heart of the issue by asking questions and pursuing leads. The other, and more common, was the time-crunched reporter who had written his or her story and needed a quote to substantiate the thesis of the piece.

The most bizarre call I remember was from a woman who worked for the Associated Press in Chicago. She first read a quote attributed to me in an alternative Chicago weekly newspaper.

"Did you say that?" she asked.

"It sounds like something I'd say."

"Well, I tried to get you to say that to me a few weeks ago, and you wouldn't."

I was speechless. Why, I wondered, would a reporter ever say that they had tried to get someone to say a particular thing and why, having said that, would they admit they were a failure? My quote opined that the current battle between chain stores and independents in Chicago was a prime example of what was happening around the country. The reporter's position had been that Chicago was the center of the battle. A subtle difference, perhaps, but certainly an important one that this reporter failed, or didn't wish, to see.

The constant buzz among independent booksellers across the country during the early '90s was about superstore rollouts and discounting. Here at home in Bellingham, we, too, were planning to expand our store and offer more value-pricing to our customers.

One of the more pleasant tasks I was asked to perform as a board member of the ABA was introducing authors. However, I don't remember ever being as nervous as I was the first time I introduced at one of our national conventions. The author breakfasts are usually attended by a thousand to fifteen hundred booksellers and publishers. I was accustomed to public speaking, but nothing quite that public.

Isabelle Allende was the first person I would introduce. I was seated next to her on the podium, and it became immediately apparent that she was very nervous. She had pushed aside her breakfast and was anxiously looking through her notes. Realizing that no one had come to see me, and noting how on edge she was, I asked her about her mother, who was sitting at one of the tables near the front of the room. She explained that when her mother Francisca was not visiting her, she began each day by writing a letter to her.

Our conversation took both of our minds away and eased our anxiety. It's unlikely that others in the room knew that we were nervous.

A year later I had the opportunity to introduce Alice Walker. Remembering my experience with Isabelle Allende, and my surprise at her nervousness, I turned to Ms. Walker and asked, "Do you ever get used to this?"

She smiled and said, "No. Just as I think I'm really relaxed, I realize my thighs have totally tightened up on me."

Introducing President Carter was the highlight of my presidential encounters. At our national convention in 1992, I'd just become president of the American Booksellers Association and was the emcee for a breakfast of about twelve hundred booksellers and publishers who had come to see the former president.

As we walked onto the stage, the room exploded in a standing ovation. As the applause continued, President Carter, with his inimitable grin, turned to me and said, "You're a very popular president."

In introducing President Carter that morning I was able to borrow a line that James Laney, President of Emory University at the time, had used just a few weeks earlier: "Jimmy Carter is the only man in history to use the U.S. Presidency as a stepping stone to serve humanity."

At our national convention in 1993, I was a participant in a panel about free speech called "The Fine Line." The event took the form of a Socratic seminar led by Harvard law professor Arthur Miller, and included a veritable who's who of authors and other well-known individuals, including Maya Angelou, Erica Jong, Judy Blume, Judge Robert Bork, Nat Hentoff, and Michael Medved. There were nineteen of us in all. I was one of only two people on the panel who was not recognized beyond that auditorium full of booksellers.

In addition to my encounter with Catharine MacKinnon, I also had the opportunity to engage with Judge Robert Bork. During a conversation about determining what speech should or should not be protected, Bork suggested that we decide by majority rule, just as we decide many other issues in civil society. I couldn't restrain myself from responding, "The First Amendment was created to protect minority speech. Majority speech is protected de facto."

Bork didn't respond, but certainly a respected law professor must have understood that.

Another notable interaction during that event involved Maya Angelou and Jack Thompson, the attorney who successfully litigated the indecency fines against 2 Live Crew for their album *As Nasty As They Wanna Be.*

"Children should be exposed to a wide variety of literature," said Angelou.

"But the question is 'what kind of literature?'" said Jack Thompson.

Thompson was nearly blown back in his chair as Maya Angelou turned to him and said, "Oh, ALL kinds of literature."

The 1993 convention in Miami is also memorable for three other encounters—a chance to introduce Stephen King, have dinner with Maya Angelou, and spend forty-five minutes with Margaret Thatcher.

Stephen King is the man the literati love to hate—or perhaps it's just jealousy. King, a former high school teacher who wrote his early books in a double-wide trailer, then a cramped apartment, as he struggled with his alcoholism, had hit the jackpot and was now earning far more than anyone who was writing "literature."

But Stephen King is one of the kindest, gentlest souls one would ever want to meet.

"Mr. King, I'm Chuck Robinson, I'll be introducing you this afternoon."

"Hello, Chuck. This is my wife, Tabby."

Tabitha King, also an author, smiled and shook my hand.

There was no sign of ego in the way King interacted with me or in the way he addressed the audience that afternoon. Like most successful authors, Tom Clancy being a notable exception, Stephen King is just a regular guy who writes books and treats others the way he, himself, likes to be treated.

If you doubt that you can feel the power of another person, you've never been in a room with Maya Angelou. Dee and I, along with a dozen or so other booksellers, were invited to have dinner with her. We had arrived early and were sipping our wine when Ms. Angelou arrived. It felt like there had been an extreme change in air pressure, and everyone seemed to sense that the person who had entered the room was a person of power—warm, benevolent power. She is definitely a presence.

Her power extends to her voice. I also had the honor of emceeing a breakfast at which she spoke. When I had introduced her, she stepped to the podium and began singing a moving African song—she speaks six languages, including West-African Fanti. Her rich, deep voice filled the room and mesmerized the audience.

Margaret Thatcher's reputation for being sexy has always puzzled me, but I must admit to having spent nearly an hour with the former British prime minister… in her hotel suite.

Mrs. Thatcher's book *The Downing Street Years* was to be published in the fall of 1993. She was a guest at the convention, and her publisher had arranged for members of the ABA board to meet Mrs. Thatcher at her hotel for a chat.

Though she was not a large woman, her presence did fill the room, and while she was very gracious and pleasant, her confidence left little doubt why she had been called the "Iron Lady."

It is always a pleasure to meet important leaders. However, by the time the hour had passed, the group was happy to escape the long account of how Mrs. Thatcher and President Reagan had saved the world for democracy. Others in the group likely shared my opinion that, while the Reagan and Thatcher administrations may have hastened the demise of the Soviet Union, the archaic and ineffective system had collapsed, in large part, under its own weight.

As the chain stores rolled out their big box stores across the country, they increasingly used discounting to establish their market share. Because low margins and relatively high operating costs had made discounting extremely difficult for independents, we chose to offer value to our customers by offering bargain books. Since those books had been a growing part of our business, in April of 1993 we took over the space on the lower level, just north of us, that Brentley Softpacks— now Brenthaven—had recently vacated. The only entry to the space was a door off the cobblestone walkway at the back. To reach the new area from the bookstore, one had to go outside and back in.

We turned this into our Bargain Book Annex. We had been selling an increasing number of remainders—usually hardcovers that publishers had marked down in price after a paperback release, or books of which publishers had significant overstocks. We needed more space to display them, and wanted to be able to free up space for other books, especially an expansion of our children's section, in the space where the remainders were currently displayed.

The Bargain Book Annex was not an attractive space. The concrete floor had been painted red, and there were several unadorned white walls that had been left, creating a rabbit warren effect. Many of the original fixtures were red cardboard tables, intended for temporary sales. But the title selection grew rapidly, as did sales, and over the next few months the store's newsletter, renamed *BookClub Banner*, carried a short list of recently added titles, including *The Living* by Annie Dillard, *Russka* by Edward Rutherford, and *Seventh Heaven* by Alice Hoffman.

The other expansion in 1993 was a joint venture with Ruby Smith and her downtown card and gift shop called Scribble. Ruby wanted to add a selection of books to her store, and joined with us to open Scribble Book Store. Ruby was the sole owner, however, though Village Books provided the inventory and consulted in the setup of the shop. The Scribble Book Store closed at the end of 1994 and Scribble closed in 1996. The February 1995 *BookClub Banner* carried the following note in announcing the closing.

We must express our deepest appreciation to Ruby Smith, owner of Scribble, and for her handyman husband (who moonlights as a dentist), Curt Smith. The enthusiasm they brought to this cooperative venture to add to the downtown core was astounding, and their patience and hard work was herculean. Scribble continues as a fine stationery, card, and gift shop—we wish them the best.

As our author events continued to grow, some crowds exceeded our capacity at the store. One of the first events to be held outside the store was with Barbara Kingsolver for *Pigs in Heaven*. We had no idea what size crowd to expect, and our choice of venues was limited.

We chose Sehome High School's Little Theater with just over two hundred seats. Tickets sales benefitted the Whatcom Literacy Council, and we were quickly sold out. No one who was there that night would ever forget it. Barbara is one of the warmest, most welcoming people we've ever met, and she made everyone feel great about coming out to support literacy.

We had picked Barbara up at SeaTac, and on the way back to Bellingham stopped at The Rhododendron Café in Skagit Valley. Alaine Borgias, our Events Coordinator at the time, joined us.

As we sat in the late afternoon sunlight on the café's patio it quickly became apparent that Barbara was exhausted from her tour. With a young daughter at home, she wasn't happy to be traveling, and it had taken its toll.

"I was walking through O'Hare the other day, the day my picture was on the front page of *USA Today*," she said. "There were racks with papers the entire length of the concourse and I just kept seeing my face. I said to myself, 'That's not Barbara Kingsolver. Barbara Kingsolver is a mother who puts her daughter to bed at night.'"

Alaine had a one-year-old son, Finnian, and fortunately the conversation shifted from the unrelenting tour to the joys and challenges of motherhood, and to the two infants. Barbara's spirits were visibly buoyed.

Had the rapid expansion of chain superstores during this period been simply the result of market forces, indie booksellers would have just had to live with it. However, information about discriminatory terms had come to the association from a number of sources—mis-mailed invoices, publisher insiders' comments, and the work of a private investigation firm. The ABA was working with some of the best anti-trust attorneys in the country and, after conducting a thorough investigation, decided to pursue the issue through legal channels.

I particularly remember one meeting in the office of our attorneys. We had worked often with a couple of the lawyers on association issues but now, as we were considering filing a lawsuit, we were introduced to a young litigator.

"I imagine you've all seen the film *Patton*," he said.

There were affirming nods around the table.

"You know that scene where Patton looks out the window on a vista of utter destruction and says, 'God help me, I love it.' Well, that's how I feel about litigation." We knew we had the right guy.

On the morning our national convention opened in 1994, ABA filed suit against five publishers—Random House, St. Martin's Press, Houghton Mifflin, Rutledge Hill Press, and Hugh Lauter Levin. The president of the publishers' association called it "a bush league action," but over the course of the next two and a half years, settlements were reached with all five publishers, all agreeing to offer the same prices and promotional terms to independents and chain stores.

"Publishers representing 40 percent of the volume of trade books in the country are now operating under a consent decree," said Bernie Rath, the association's executive director, when the last settlement was reached in November of 1996.

Nearly a year later, following an investigation of a possible violation of the court-monitored consent decree, Penguin Group USA settled with the ABA for $25 million. Jerald Jacobs, the association's attorney, said the settlement was "by far the largest antitrust discrimination settlement ever in the over-60-year history of the antitrust discrimination laws."

ABA distributed one half of the money to its members, based on their purchases from Penguin. Any ABA member bookstore that could prove the purchase of just one Penguin book during the period outlined in the settlement was sent $1000. Stores that could document larger volume purchases received settlements based on those purchases. Village Books received a check for $13,782. The other half of the settlement was retained by ABA to use to serve its members.

In March of 1998, shortly before the Penguin settlement,

the ABA and twenty-six independent booksellers sued Barnes & Noble and Borders for bullying publishers into providing discriminatory discounts. Although Village Books was not a plaintiff in the suit, we did confer with the association's attorneys and strongly support the litigation. That suit was finally settled on April 19, 2001, with the defendants paying ABA $4.7 million.

It was, however, a hollow victory for independent booksellers, since the association had spent $16 million trying the case, and plaintiffs were denied damages. The defendants spent an estimated $75 million dollars. While the ABA felt the ruling could be overturned on appeal, the board decided, because of the cost and the time it would likely take, not to pursue it.

A positive result of both lawsuits was the leveling of the playing field for indies and chains. How level that field is today is an unanswered question.

During the spring and early summer of 1994, the Bargain Book Annex was totally remodeled. In the July *BookClub Banner* we announced:

Over the past few months we have been remodeling the Bargain Book Annex. Now, with the exception of a few trim pieces here and some paint touch-ups there, the project is completed. With new carpeting, paint, shelving, and lights, the Bargain Book Annex now feels like a place where you (and we) would like to spend some time.

Along with the remodel we added a second entrance to the Annex by opening the doorway on Eleventh Street that led down a stairway, past a boulder that had been left unexcavated in the floor, and into the area where we were displaying our bargain books. The remodel had also created a much roomier and more comfortable area for our Literature Live programs. One still could not enter directly from the main part of the bookstore—it would be another year before that became possible.

The biggest expansion that summer was not physical. On July 1st, 1994, Village Books began buying and selling used books. For years our friend Michael Powell of Powell's Books in Portland had harangued us about how crazy it was for us not to be selling used books. That spring I called Mike and told him Jim Speidel and I would like to come down and learn about buying and selling used books. Powell's had recently designed a training session for other booksellers, who would pay a fee to spend three days learning different aspects of the used books business.

Jim and I, along with a bookseller from New Mexico, took the training course, and over three intensely packed days learned a wealth of information about the business, much of which still guides the way we operate today. But two single pieces of information convinced us to add used books: 1) Powell's demonstrated that buying and selling used books was not rocket science, and 2) they persuaded us that we already knew far more about used books than we thought we did. We began buying and shelving used books with the remainders, arranged by sections throughout the Bargain Book Annex. We continued to sell used and bargain books from the Annex for the next ten years, until the new store was built.

Meanwhile, the censorship warriors marched on. In 1994 Cathy Mickels led the battle against Jane Smiley's book *1000 Acres* at Lynden High School. Carole Hanaway was using the book in an advanced-placement English class and, after a parental complaint, the curriculum-advisory committee, composed of teachers, administrators, and parents had voted to keep the book. Apparently worried about a pending school bond vote, Principal Ken Axelson, who had originally approved the book's use, announced that it was being dropped. Nonetheless, the bond issue failed.

Once again, the banning of a book led to increased sales and considerable discussion throughout the area, and across the country. While those opposed to the book's use in the high school cited sexual scenes, some of us suspect that the fear of a discussion of sexual abuse might have been a prime motivator.

The book business was keeping us moving. Though we had once thought we might have only one trip to Europe, things have turned out quite differently. Two years after our grand tour, as president of ABA I attended the International Federation of Booksellers (IBF) meeting in Bruges, Belgium. IBF is primarily a European organization with a few members in the U.S., Canada, and elsewhere, but ABA has been a regular participant in its meetings.

Dee and I flew into Amsterdam and were able to spend a couple of days viewing Van Goghs and Rembrandts, visiting Anne Frank's home, and generally seeing the sights. The train allowed a short layover in Brussels for some sightseeing before arriving in Bruges, where we enjoyed the art and architecture within the walls of the medieval city for five days. After the conference, we went on to Paris for a week.

The next year the British Booksellers Association flew me to Jersey to speak at their convention. Before the meetings we spent two days in Normandy and Brittany, including a night at Mont St. Michel. After the meetings we took a three-week driving trip up the west side of England, with a brief dip into Wales and Scotland and back down the east side to London.

London taught us an important lesson about pre-judgements. We knew there were many great things to see, but, for reasons I can't quite explain, we didn't think we would like the city itself. We were certainly wrong about that. We somehow hadn't realized that, rather than being a huge sprawling metropolis, London is a collection of small villages that invite exploration and discovery, and we spent some time doing both. Fortunately, we would return.

ABA, with funding from George Soros' foundation, had been presenting booksellers schools in Eastern Europe, and the Soros Open Society office in Macedonia was interested in exploring the possibility of having a school presented there. I was to go to Skopje in the fall of 1994 to assess the possibilities for a school.

I had just given several presentations for the Mid-South Booksellers Association at their fall meeting in New Orleans, before boarding a plane for the long journey to Macedonia. After a layover in Frankfurt and a quick touchdown in Lubijana, I arrived on Monday evening in Skopje to be met by Mary Frances, who worked in Soros' New York office, and a couple of her Macedonian colleagues.

Macedonia had declared its independence from Yugoslavia just three years earlier, and independent publishing and bookselling was still in a fledgling state. The task Mary Frances and I faced was to talk with publishers and booksellers, and to decide whether a booksellers school would be valuable for them. If the answer was yes, Dee and I would return the next spring to conduct the school.

Skopje was an odd mix of sights. A devastating flood and earthquake in the early 1960s had destroyed most of the beautiful neoclassical buildings in the city. Sadly, many of those structures were replaced with massive Soviet-style concrete buildings, and only a small part of the old city remains.

The isolation of Macedonia, economic conditions at the time, and a lack of "book culture" conspired to create a bleak publishing and bookselling landscape. Over the course of four days, as Mary Frances and I visited with locals, I vacillated between thinking that a booksellers school could be valuable or a total waste of time.

On Saturday we drove to an area just outside Ohrid to see the site where the school would likely be held. Legend has it that Ohrid once had 365 churches, one for each day of the year. While that number is smaller now, many of those churches still stand, including Sveti Naum, a monastery built in 905. The chapel is on the eastern shore of Lake Ohrid, looking across to Albania. The area, in stark contrast to Skopje, had the feel of a Mediterranean resort.

After spending a week considering the possibilities and difficulties of conducting a booksellers school there, I returned home and wrote a report suggesting we go forward. Dee and I were scheduled to go to Ohrid the following spring. Unfortunately, the entire Soros funding model changed, and the school never happened.

Some bright ideas we've had over the years haven't always worked out. For one of the early store anniversary celebrations, we had created an interesting reward scheme. With each purchase we would give customers coins, which could then be used to purchase some special item. It was so complicated that neither customers, nor those working in the store, understood it.

In the summer of 1994, in an attempt to catch the two-times-a-week Alaska Ferry traffic, the bookstore (hoping to sell more books) and the Colophon Café (hoping to serve more breakfasts) began opening at 7 am, Monday through Saturday. I have no idea what we were thinking. Neither did our customers. We even offered a free latté or or "Mega Muffin" at the Colophon with a minimum $5 purchase before 10 am. We did get a lot of work done on those quiet mornings, but very little business was transacted.

Occasionally those missteps aren't limited just to our store.

In the early '90s the entire publishing and bookselling industry believed that interactive books on CD-Rom were going to be the next big thing. Some might remember a rack of those CD-Roms in the store. With very few exceptions, they remained on the rack.

Richard Bach had signed copies of *The Bridge Across Forever* for more than four hours in May of 1984, and had returned to talk about his new book, *Running From Safety*, ten years later. Early that November afternoon I chatted with a young couple in the store. I learned they weren't local and asked where they lived.

"Southwest Utah," the man said.

"Do you know Richard Bach will be here tonight?" I said.

"Yes, we're planning to be there."

"Great, I'll see you there."

That evening I nodded to the couple across the room. I thought this was great serendipity—a couple passing through town had happened on a reading by Richard Bach. Then came the question and answer session. The young man raised his hand and thanked Bach for his books.

"My wife and I saw on the internet that you were going to be here and drove from southwest Utah," he said.

So much for a couple passing through town.

"Thank you. What brought you so far?" asked Bach.

"When I was eighteen years old I was ready to stick a shotgun in my mouth. Then someone handed me *Jonathan Livingston Seagull*," he said. "I decided life was worth living." His wife squeezed his hand.

Have you ever doubted that books can change lives?

Chuck with more, and less gray, hair

"We're Adding Thousands of Stories to this Building" sign before VB opening

Dawn Wetherby, Dee and Abbe Rolnick shelve books during VB's move-in to second location in 1982

Chuck, Krista and Dee at 1984 VB anniversary party

Athena, the bookstore cat, napping on the counter

Mayor Tim Douglas cuts the ribbon for Colophon grand opening as Chuck and Dee and Ray and Taimi look on, June 20, 1985

View of VB's second location from mezzanine office

President Reagan welcomes Chuck to the White House
("Yes, it's the real Reagan; it's a cardboard cutout of Chuck,"
- Krista Hunter)

Chuck conducting a class at Singapore booksellers school

Staff photo, 1988, in new lower level space

Chuck takes information from friend Tom Robinson at 1988 anniversary party

Chuck talking with President George and First Lady Barbara Bush about ABFFE and the First Amendment

Cover boy Chuck when he became ABA president

VB Staff at an anniversary party in the early '90s

President Jimmy Carter, Chuck and publisher Dan Haldeman at ABA convention, 1992

Chuck presenting books to President Clinton in the Oval Office

Chuck meets British Prime Minister Margaret Thatcher

Chuck, Newt Gingrich, and Dee at convention dinner

Chuck introducing Newt Gingrich and Linda Wertheimer at "Power Lunch"

Dee and Chuck beside Lanny Little's bookmobile portrait

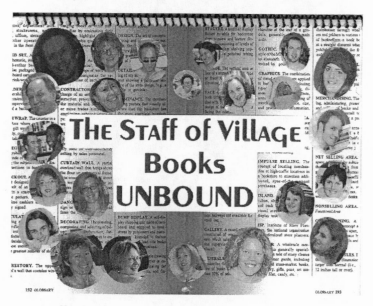

Staff calendar given to Chuck & Dee, January 2004

New Village Books building under construction, 2004

Chuck, Dee and Krista confer during new building move-in

Joe Young and Chuck Dingee of The Walrus with Rich Donnelly and Chuck at 1st Chuckanut Radio Hour

Barbara Hoenselaar, Patti Pattee, Chuck, Dee, and Christin Evans in London for book fair

Garrison Keillor and Chuck after Chuckanut Radio Hour,
September, 2008

Chuck and Dee accept the WA State Outstanding Philanthropic
Small Business Award

Chapter 6

And the Beat Goes On
1995–1999

One of the most visible and controversial local censorship cases began in January of 1995 when a complaint was filed against the Newsstand, a Bellingham magazine and newspaper shop, for carrying a publication called *Answer Me*. The magazine, or "zine," used satire to focus on rape. Earlier editions of the publication had dealt with suicide, murder, and serial killers in the same manner.

The Newsstand did take the magazine off sale, but created a protest display with the remaining copies chained. Two signs accompanied the magazines. One simply said "Not for Sale" and the other bore a quote from Jefferson, "Our liberty depends on freedom of the press and cannot be limited without being lost," and went on to explain the reason for the magazines being locked up: "Due to an anonymous complaint lodged with the Whatcom County Prosecutor's office about the contents of this issue of *Answer Me*, we have decided to place all remaining copies of this magazine under symbolic lock and key. While we sympathize with the individuals who take offense at a particular article or image, we feel that removing this magazine sets a dangerous precedent that truly threatens our ability to exist as a store as well as all of our first amendment rights."

In a meeting more than a month after the initial complaint, county prosecutor Dave McEachran threatened the owner Ira Stohl and his manager Kristina Hjelsand with arrest unless they agreed to remove the display and never sell *Answer Me* or any "similar material." Stohl and Hjelsand, believing that the magazine contained serious political content and that McEachran's demand constituted prior restraint, refused.

Fewer than a dozen copies of the magazine had been sold before being chained. A few more were given to the press and to legal counsel but, all told, the number of copies in circulation in Whatcom County was likely fewer than twenty. When I agreed to be a witness in the case I was given one of the copies, which I read cover to cover. The material was disturbing and the language was crude, but it was clear that this was not meant to titillate. Nor by any stretch of the imagination did it meet the definition of obscene.

At trial the magazine was found not to be obscene. With Hjelsand and Stohl's attention diverted to defending themselves, and the bad publicity that had been generated around the magazine, the Newsstand's business was hurt badly. And, in spite of much pro bono legal work, the case had been very expensive for the store.

The Newsstand brought suit against the prosecutor's office for damaging their business, and the case was moved to Seattle where I was, once again, a witness. Trying to prove that their business losses were not due to the *Answer Me* case, the attorney from the prosecutor's office asked me, "Mr. Robinson, isn't it true that during the time that the Newsstand's business declined, all of downtown Bellingham's businesses were suffering?" I was reminded of the old legal saw that one should never ask a question in court for which one does not know the answer. The attorney was wrong. It had, in fact, been a bit of a boom time for downtown Bellingham. A number of new businesses had opened, including a restaurant adjacent to the Newsstand, and the downtown was in a strong "comeback" mode.

The looks on faces of the jury when I gave my reply may have telegraphed their decision in the case. They ordered the county to pay the Newsstand 1.3 million dollars, but the amount was reduced on appeal to $720,000. While that may seem like a lot of money to some, it didn't make up for the cost to the business.

At the time of the case, the Newsstand carried about 5000 magazines. By contrast, our store has never carried more than 300, so we often referred folks downtown for particular publications. On numerous occasions a person would reply, "I won't shop there."

Though I suspected their reasons, I would usually ask, "Why is that?"

"I won't shop somewhere that carries magazines like that," they said. Knowing that it was unlikely that they'd ever seen the magazine in question, I would occasionally pursue the subject and ask what kind of materials they were talking about. Most had no idea of the nature of *Answer Me*, and made assumptions based on the fact that the prosecutor had brought charges.

Though the Newsstand remained in business until 2008, it's not clear that they ever fully recovered from the incident.

"And the Speaker left speechless."

That's what the commentator said on "Hard Copy," the nationally syndicated news tabloid TV program, the evening after the "Power Lunch" at the ABA Convention in Chicago in June of 1995. The guests on the program that noon were NPR's Linda Wertheimer, Ben Bradlee of *The Washington Post* and Newt Gingrich, the Speaker of the House to whom the commentator referred. I was the moderator.

Gingrich was just beginning a tour for his book *To Renew America*, Wertheimer was there to talk about her forthcoming book *Listening to America*, and Bradlee would talk about his book *A Good Life*.

But all didn't go as planned. An Associated Press story had this to say after mentioning that Gingrich was the featured speaker (which was not accurate, given that there were three "featured" speakers):

"But some strange things happened on the way to the podium. First, the man who introduced him, former ABA president Chuck Robinson, read an association statement supporting federal funding of the arts. Some Republicans in Congress are trying to cut such funding, and Gingrich has hinted that he supports the effort.

Then, just as Gingrich started speaking, a heckler began shouting about proposed cuts in social programs. A few more hecklers soon emerged, delaying the speech several minutes until security led them away. The hecklers were local activists who had gotten in by purchasing tickets."

As the AP story says, the speech was delayed several minutes, but the Speaker did not leave speechless as the hyperbolic "Hard Copy" commentator had suggested. Gingrich did give his entire speech and was even heartily applauded for praising America's tolerance of dissent.

Every network had cameras in the room, and that evening numerous news programs carried the story, though no other account, to my knowledge, was as inaccurate as that given on "Hard Copy." If I had been skeptical of TV news before the incident, you can be certain my skepticism had now risen to new heights.

"Nobody goes there anymore, it's too crowded."

That, of course, is a famous Yogi Berra line that seems to apply to the parking situation in Fairhaven.

There have been complaints about parking in Fairhaven for most of the thirty years we've been here. People's perceptions and expectations about parking shift wildly, depending on the context. No one complains about parking three blocks away from his or her destination when going to Seattle, nor, for that matter, do they measure how far away from a desired store they park when shopping at a mall.

A few years ago a friend told me of sitting one day in the front window of Tony's watching the world pass by. While he sat there he saw a car come down Harris heading west, turn right heading north on 11th Street, and disappear from his view. All of the time the driver was obviously looking for a parking spot. In a short time the same car reappeared driving west down Harris, and once again turned north on 11th while continuing its quest. My friend watched the same car circle the block five times. Little did the driver know—and signing certainly would have helped—that, had he turned left on 11th and headed south one block, he would have driven into parking Nirvana in the form of the McKenzie parking lot.

It would be wrong to say there have not been parking problems. By 1995, as more businesses opened in the district, it was sometimes difficult to find a place to park. However, with the formation of a parking district, McKenzie Avenue between 10th and 12th Streets was converted to parking, while still allowing traffic to flow through. By spring 1996, more parking was being created along Mill Avenue between 10th and 11th Streets and on 10th Street between Mill and Harris. The addition of those parking areas alleviated many of the issues of finding a place to leave one's car and, to this day, places are almost always open in the McKenzie lot.

The crunch on parking spaces returned with the beginning of the Fairhaven construction boom in 2004. Workers and construction equipment occupied many spaces on weekdays. While more spaces opened up on weekends, it's likely that some folks, having searched for a place during the week, might not have known that and avoided Fairhaven altogether. As construction wound down a few years later, parking once again opened up.

Though it will be important to address future parking needs, I'm also hopeful that public transportation and bicycles— many bike racks have been added in the past few years—will help with this as well. A couple of years ago I checked out the McKenzie lot at 2:15 on a busy Saturday afternoon, with cafés full and shop aisles crowded. There were nineteen empty spots. That number might be smaller today—though, with the current economic troubles, perhaps not—but at the busiest times there are still spots available, many within two hundred steps from our door.

In the fall of 1995 an interior connection to the Bargain Book Annex was finally created. A dust room of vinyl sheeting was built on each side of the wall separating the Annex from the Colophon, and a two-man crew came in each night at closing, worked through the night, and had the area cleaned up before opening time the next morning. When she bid the job, the estimator scratched the mortar holding together the large blocks of Chuckanut sandstone, and it flaked away quite easily. As the workmen began the demolition they discovered that, below the surface, the mortar was as hard as the stone itself. The wall was built like old castles with two courses of stone and rubble in the center. It was more than three feet thick in one spot, and took a long time to demolish. The estimator later told us that we were fortunate they gave us a fixed price.

The two guys who worked on the project were terrific. Each night when they came in we would talk and joke with them, and then we would see them in the mornings as they were leaving. They took great pains not to disrupt our business and they were so proud of their work that on the Gallery Walk night on the Friday after Thanksgiving, when the doorway was first open, they both brought their wives to the store to show them what they had done. One of the men, Tom Luther, was the superintendent when our new building was built eight and a half years later, and he still remembered the doorway project quite well.

Shortly after the opening was complete a regular customer came in and commented, "I really like your new door. I'll bet you wish you'd done it earlier."

"We planned to do it a year and a half ago with the Annex remodel, but we ran out of money," I said.

"I bet you wish you'd done it first," he said.

He was right, of course. Foot traffic into the Annex increased exponentially and sales of used and bargain books soared as well. It was also much easier to get folks into readings and into the store after readings. We likely should have done it earlier, but as the company told us when the job was finished, "You'll be pleased to know that these are the most expensive doors we've ever installed."

Terry Tempest Williams has always mesmerized audiences. At a reading for *Desert Quartet*, fifteen years ago, everyone sat in silence for ten minutes after she finished reading, stepped back from the podium, and bowed her head.

"It just seemed that long," a friend said when I told him about it.

"I was standing next to the clock," I insisted.

At the end of the event I walked up to long-time staff member Mitchell Moore, whose picture, I've often joked, should appear as the definition of cynic in the dictionary.

"Well, that's the closest thing to a religious experience I've had in a long time," he said.

After the reading a handful of us sat around and talked with Terry and her dad John, who was traveling with her. John is a tall, lean, ruggedly handsome man—the epitome of the quiet, modern cowboy. He was in his sixties at the time, and several of the women in the audience, learning he was a widower, had given him their names and phone numbers. As we sat and chatted, the conversation turned to Terry's book *Refuge*.

"I had a really hard time with that book," John said. "I'm a business man who plays his cards close to the vest, and she revealed a lot about me in the book. She made me seem stubborn."

Terry rolled her eyes.

Knowing that some themes recur often in families, Dee said, "This sounds like a conversation that's happened before."

"No, not really," said Terry.

A couple of years later, speaking at our regional booksellers meeting, Terry was acknowledging and thanking particular booksellers in the room.

"I'd like to thank Chuck and Dee from Village Books in Bellingham, where my father believes he's going to find a wife," she said.

When Terry's husband Brooke published his book *Half Lives: Reconciling Work and Wilderness*, he told Terry's dad that he would be doing a reading at Village Books.

"I'd really like to go with you and support you," John said.

When Brooke told Terry how sweet it was that her dad wanted to support his work, Terry laughed and said, "Bull, he just thinks he's going to meet a woman there."

In January of 2009 Terry filled the Congregational Church when she talked about her book *Finding Beauty in a Broken World*. It was a kick-off event for Whatcom Land Trust's silver anniversary. Her long association with land trusts became clear as she talked not only about her book but also about the importance of the work that Whatcom Land Trust was doing in our area. Terry left no dry eyes in the house in her explanation of the book that ties together the art of mosaic, the extinction of prairie dogs, and the genocide in Rwanda. We had seen the same reaction in a packed Benaroya Hall in Seattle a few months before.

After her presentation at the church she spent untold time with each person who approached her. I have never seen Terry engage in a superficial conversation with anyone. No one listens or empathizes like she does. That evening, like any time spent with Terry Tempest Williams, will long last in the memories of all who were there.

Sherman Alexie began coming to Village Books in 1991 with the publication of his first book of poetry, *The Business of Fancy Dancing*. By the time *Reservation Blues* was published in 1995 the crowds that came to see him had outgrown our Readings Gallery and we hosted him at Fairhaven Middle School. That evening Sherman nearly had the show stolen from him by Cha-da-ska-dum Which-ta-lum, a Lummi elder. Cha-da-ska-dum was a giant of a man with a laugh that matched his size. Sherman is capable of eliciting belly laughs from nearly everyone, but everyone doesn't have a belly like Cha-da-ska-dum's.

During one particularly funny part of the program, Cha-da-ska-dum began laughing and just couldn't stop. Sherman paused, turned in his direction and, with a big grin on his face, said, "Who is that guy? I'm taking him with me on tour." Moments later, when Cha-sa-ska-dum erupted in yet another fit of laughter, Sherman said, "I'm serious. I'm calling my publisher and telling him this guy's going with me. He's Indian. It's affirmative action."

In the *Chuckanut Reader* celebrating our fifteenth anniversary, we published this piece that Sherman wrote about the store:

Independent bookstores are proof of God. I don't mean that in some mushy kind of way. I mean that in a tough way, like an Old Testament God, full of disaster and dark imagery, hard-earned redemption and gentle forgiveness. Independent bookstores feed us all.

Now, Village Books, there's a bookstore I wish I could ask to dance. I'd walk up to the store, shyly, or at least, pretending to be shy, and say, 'Hey, you're an attractive bookstore.' Then, after I carefully and secretly checked the smell of my breath, I'd lean in close and whisper, 'How would you like to dance?' Village Books is the kind of store that would smile, nod its head, and lead me onto the dance floor. The dancing would be good, something slow and easy to begin with, and then a sudden shift in rhythm, until we were hopping up and down like crazy rabbits.

Sherman has since outgrown spaces the size of Fairhaven Middle School as well. On several occasions he's packed the 800-seat auditorium at Bellingham High School, and as the first author selected by Whatcom Reads for the county-wide reading and discussion program, brought two large audiences to the Whatcom Community College pavilion in one day.

In addition to those two talks, he also appeared at two high schools, the juvenile detention center, Western Washington University, and had dinner with a group of young writers. His generosity was unlimited and his interaction with everyone, from the Whatcom Reads committee to students to the many adults who talked with him at events, was warm and welcoming.

Sherman is everything readers and independent booksellers could wish for in a writer—great stories, well told; strong, sometimes cutting opinions; a great sense of humor; but, most of all, a humanity that transcends all. We're thrilled that he has become such a big part of our bookstore family.

Early in the summer of 1996 I received a call from the United States Information Agency (USIA). Though the agency had long maintained ties with the CIA, the call wasn't about spying. It was about propaganda—propaganda in its best sense, the *Webster's Dictionary* sense: "any systematic, widespread dissemination or promotion of particular ideas, doctrines, practices, etc. to further one's own cause..." "One's own cause," in this case, was the protection of copyright and intellectual property rights, and I was being asked to travel to Jordan and Israel as part of the USIA's Corridors of Culture program, to talk about their importance.

I would be joined by poet, novelist, and travel writer Colleen McElroy, who was teaching at the University of Washington, and Lawrence Jordan, a New York literary agent. Did I want to go, and did I know anyone in publishing who should be on this excursion? I didn't hesitate. A trip to the Middle East, including Jerusalem, had long been on my dream list. And my friend Richard Hunt, at Bantam Doubleday Dell in New York City, seemed a perfect fit for the publisher slot. I quickly agreed to go and pointed them toward Richard.

A few nights later, at nine o'clock, I answered a call at the store and heard, "Hello, Chuck, it's Richard." He was calling from his office, having gone back in, as he often did, to do some late night work.

I answered, "Richard, did USIA call you?"

"Yes, but do you think it's safe to go to the Middle East?"

"Wait a minute, you're calling me from Times Square at midnight to ask if it's safe to go to the Middle East?"

After a brief pause came his response, "Okay, I get it." Richard agreed to become part of the team.

A few weeks before we were scheduled to leave for the Middle East, troubles broke out in Ramallah, and the USIA changed our itinerary from Israel to Morocco.

We arrived in Amman, Jordan, late on Sunday afternoon, October 6th, and were whisked off to the Marriott Hotel. Though it was exciting to be there, it was also frustrating to think that we were only an hour's drive from Jerusalem and there was no way to see the city that gave birth to three major world religions. After a full night's rest and a typical Middle Eastern breakfast of olives, hummus, pita bread, meats, and fruit, we began our orientation to the country and the publishing and intellectual scene with a briefing from the in-country USIA staff.

That afternoon we met with H.R.H. Prince Ghazi Bin

Mohammed, Cultural Advisor to His Majesty King Hussein—and the king's nephew. When we entered his office the prince was in typical western business attire, and he quickly made us feel at home. As a person who had published a book, the prince was very interested in our mission and eager to talk with us about it. After finishing the formal conversation, Richard, acknowledging the prince's Princeton education, asked, "Are there any things you miss about the U.S.?"

"There are many things I miss."

"Well," asked Richard, "what do you miss most?"

"Philly cheesesteak sandwiches."

Prince Ghazi was so interested in our program that he asked if we might join him, at the end of our week there, at his country home near the Dead Sea. It took no arm-twisting on his part to get us to agree, and we spent much of the rest of the week thinking about our Sunday journey.

Tuesday through Thursday was a whirlwind of activity—a seminar at Jordan University's Faculty of Arts, a meeting with the Jordanian Writers Federation, a lovely reception at the home of the USIA Public Affairs Officer, meetings with the Jordanian Publishers Union and Jordanian Writers Union, a presentation to the Amman Rotary, a TV taping at Jordan Television Studios, a literary luncheon with Jordanian writers and literary figures, and a reading by Colleen at Amman Bookstore.

It's difficult to describe the woman who was our escort from the U.S. office of USIA. Suffice it to say it often seemed like she would rather be anywhere else. She was brusque with us and very demanding. Her manner likely formed an even tighter bond among the four of us, who had quickly discovered that we liked each other and weren't that fond of her. At one point she had asked all of us to entrust her with our return airline tickets. Feeling somewhat insulted—we were, after all, adults—we declined.

On the evening of Colleen's bookstore reading, I had a distinct notion that I should have handed mine over. On returning to the hotel I couldn't find my ticket folder anywhere. I searched my bag, my clothes, the entire room. No ticket. In a panic I called Richard, who came to my room and helped me repeat the search, to no avail.

"Richard, the ticket's on the back floor of the van," I suddenly exclaimed, remembering that I had draped my sport coat over the van's back seat with the ticket in the inside pocket.

"Call the woman from the embassy," he said. We had her home number in case of an emergency.

"This is Chuck Robinson," I said with some trepidation. "I think my plane ticket is on the floor of the van. Is there any way to get it? And, please, don't let Carolyn know."

In less than two hours, though it seemed much longer, the driver arrived, and with a smile, handed over my ticket and repeatedly refused the tip I offered him. Relief coursed through my entire body.

Though it was deeply disappointing not to be going to Jerusalem, we knew we would be going to Morocco and would also have an extra day in Jordan to see Petra. It was a long and dusty drive—nearly 200 miles—but it was certainly worth it. Petra, meaning cleft in the rock in Greek, was described by Pliny the Elder and other writers as the capital of the Aramaic-speaking Nabataeans, who used the perpetually-watered site as a center for their caravan trade. It's known by most Americans as the site of the Temple housing the Holy Grail from the Indiana Jones movie.

We spent the night of October 11th in the Bedouin-style Taybet Zaman hotel, just five miles from the entrance to Petra. It was Dee's birthday and the first time in more than thirty years that we hadn't celebrated together. Talking on the phone was some consolation, but it really would have been a great place to celebrate together.

We hiked through Petra the next day. Even the extravagant cinematic treatment in *Indiana Jones and the Last Crusade* hadn't done it justice. It was hard to imagine an ancient people hand-chiseling these elaborately detailed temples, houses, banquet halls, and tombs into the red sandstone cliffs.

When Sunday arrived we once again took a desert drive, this time to the country home of Prince Ghiza. It was, surprisingly, a modest dwelling in a suburban-like cluster of houses, and was mostly distinguished from the neighboring homes by the soldiers with Uzis in the driveway. This time the prince was wearing the more traditional dishdasha (robe) and keffiyeh (head scarf). He welcomed us into his home, served traditional Jordanian food, and then donned hiking boots and took us to see a stone building that Solomon built, and a great view of the Dead Sea. It was a wonderful way to end our time in Jordan.

When our plane arrived in Casablanca on Monday afternoon, we were met by a driver who took us immediately to Marrakesh for a day of relaxation and sightseeing. There we met our guide, a middle-aged man whose knowledge of American literature rivaled ours.

He toured us around the city, pointing out current sights and telling us historically important facts. Our visit to the souk with its amazing abundance of goods, rainbow of colors, and array of sounds and smells was the highlight of our visit to this once imperial city.

On Tuesday we returned to Casablanca and five days of presentations there and in Rabat that mirrored those in Jordan, including a late night dinner at the home of the Minister of Culture. Though it was once again a whirlwind of events, we did have time to take in some important sights.

The highlight in Casablanca was the Hassan II Mosque.

It's the third largest mosque in the world, after those in Mecca and Medina. Its minaret is the world's tallest, and the building can accommodate 25,000 worshippers inside and another 80,000 on the grounds.

After a final presentation in Rabat, we flew off to Paris for an afternoon and evening of R&R, catching a Picasso portraits show at the Grand Palais and dining together at Brasserie de l'Isle Saint Louis, then returned home the next day with memories to last a lifetime.

Occasionally booksellers are asked to read a book in manuscript and, if they like it, provide a blurb for the jacket. Knowing that I was a huge Ivan Doig fan, Simon & Schuster asked if I would read the manuscript of *Bucking the Sun*. I did, and I loved it. I provided this quote that was used as a jacket blurb:

I have long felt about Ivan Doig's books much as Will Rogers must have felt about his fellow human beings–I've never met one I didn't like. But I've never read one I liked more than *Bucking the Sun*. Doig has concentrated the full force of his immense writing talents and his bone-deep feel for the Big Sky country on telling this epic tale. Nowhere are fictional characters so fully alive. Nowhere do events long past seem so present. This is Ivan Doig at his best, and writing just doesn't get any better.

– Chuck Robinson, Past President of the
American Booksellers Association

In fact, I was so in love with the book that we decided to produce, through an agreement with the publisher, two sets of limited editions of the book—to date, the only Doig limiteds ever published. One set consisted of twenty-six signed and lettered books, bound in leather and slipcased. The other, signed and numbered in an edition of one hundred fifty, was bound in bonded leather and slipcased.

Ivan, like Sherman Alexie, also wrote a very nice piece for our fifteenth anniversary:

'Home, Home, I knew it entering,' runs the opening line of Richard Hugo's heartsome poem 'The Only Bar in Dixon,' and although Village Books is naturally of higher literary pedigree, it too is a treasured oasis, one of a kind, and has provided intoxicating times. Where but there have I ever inscribed a book to Jackpine Judy—'That's my wife,' explained the blushing young man in the lumberjack shirt, 'and, uh, can you add to Pinecone Pete, that's me.' Where else do the booklovers come down from Western and up from the waterfront and in from the hills around–doing a reading in Bellingham is like no other audience I open a book to; the mix of people, the cocked heads of attention, empathy, understanding. Well, I very nearly knew it entering, having done my first of I don't know how many appearances at Village Books in its opening year of 1980, and I hope to be saying this same thing for at least its next 15 years: Village Books, Chuck and Dee Robinson, their staff—if they didn't exist, we couldn't invent them.

Robert Gates is the only career officer in the CIA's history to rise from entry-level employee to Director. When he came to Village Books in 1996 to present his book *Out of the Shadows*, most people expected he would talk at length about his experience in the CIA. Though he did mention his twenty-seven year career as an intelligence professional, he spent much more time exploring a wide range of policy issues and international relations.

When asked in the question and answer period about his thoughts on the recently-elected Israeli Prime Minister Benjamin Netanyahu, Gates said, "I think it's the worst thing that could have happened to Israel." His view of Netanyahu dated from a White House visit during the time Gates was the Deputy National Security Adviser to President George H. W. Bush. He considered Netanyahu extremely arrogant and remembered, after he left, turning to National Security Advisor Brent Scowcroft and saying, "That man should never be allowed back in the White House."

He was also asked about the upcoming Russian presidential elections. He spoke knowledgeably about the incumbent Boris Yeltsin and his challenger Gennady Zyuganov. He also commented on Mikhail Gorbachev's policies of reform (perestroika) and new freedoms (glasnost) and the situation in which Gorbachev found himself presiding over the collapse of the Soviet Union. The evening turned into one of the most interesting civics and history lessons I've ever had.

At a small reception at a mutual friend's home, Mr. Gates, whose new home was at Big Lake in Skagit County, was asked about the rumor that he would run for office in Washington State. Gates laughed and said, "I've worked for six Presidents and I've seen enough politics. In fact, the only person I'd go back to D.C. for is Colin Powell." Powell had recently announced that he would not seek the presidency, a decision that Gates said was "a good personal decision but a loss for the country."

Mr. Gates obviously changed his mind about returning to D.C. On December 18, 2006, he was sworn into the George W. Bush administration as the 22nd U.S. Secretary of Defense, and became the first in history to be asked to remain in office by a newly elected President—Barack Obama.

Salman Rushdie had been scheduled to speak at Elliott Bay Book Company in Seattle on March 9th of 1989, but cancelled his tour after the fatwa was announced. Seven years later I received a phone call from a woman at Seattle Arts and Lectures.

"Salman Rushdie will be speaking at the First United Methodist Church on January 23," she said. "SAL subscribers are being sent invitations, and you're being invited as a member of the bookselling community. You're also invited to a reception at Campagne following the event."

She told me that this must be kept secret and that if word got out, the event would be cancelled. According to book critic Michael Upchurch in a *Seattle Times* article, SAL members received "mysteriously worded invitations" that promised only that "a literary luminary would turn up." The press had apparently been notified as well, but were likewise asked not to spread the word.

A thousand people arrived that rainy evening and waited in a serpentine line outside the church to pass through metal detectors. The secrecy that had been maintained was not lost on Rushdie who, according to Upchurch, said, "Somehow a thousand people managed to keep a secret, which I thought was very impressive."

When we were invited to the reception I hadn't given any thought to the venue and had assumed there might be several hundred people in attendance. As we approached Campagne Restaurant, a place where we had attended many publisher dinners, it occurred to me that it was too small for a large group. Rather than hundreds, only about thirty people had been invited.

In contrast to the security at the church, the restaurant was still open, with a number of diners still finishing their meals, and no one seemed to be concerned about who entered. When we walked in, there was Rushdie, standing near the bar, nonchalantly chatting with folks.

We were directed to the back dining room, where we sipped wine as Rushdie moved from table to table, spending considerable time with each small group. At our table we talked with him about literature, U.S. and British politics, and the seven years he had spent in seclusion. This was certainly one of my greatest "just pinch me" experiences.

When *Whatcom Places* was published in the late spring of 1997, it was the first time there had been a big, color photo book of the area. Beyond that, it contained thoughtful essays about nearly every natural aspect of our local environment. But most impressive was that it was a monument to one of the most collaborative publishing efforts I've ever seen.

Bob Keller, a retired Fairhaven College professor and extremely active board member of the Whatcom Land Trust, had seen a publication from the San Juan Preservation Trust and wanted to create a similar publication for the local organization. The piece he showed me was a beautiful, staple-bound, thirty-six page booklet.

Bob's plan was to raise money from donors to publish an educational booklet like theirs. Because there was not a beautiful photo book of the area, there was great potential for a book that could be sold to many people. That would further the Land Trust's goals, which were: 1) To create more awareness of and appreciation for the Whatcom landscape. 2) To develop a classy, useful tool for the Land Trust to publicize its mission. 3) To portray the diversity of the landscape as well as a diversity of points of view about it.

A book committee was put in place in March of 1996. Speaking about the process upon publication of the book, just over a year later, Bob said: "The book committee began with a community organizing miracle—after one hour of phoning, everyone I asked to serve had agreed!"

I was fortunate to be one of those committee members, offering publishing and marketing advice in cooperation with other members of the group. I also recruited Ivan Doig to write the book's introduction, "A Sense of Place."

The collaborative effort didn't end there. According to Bob, "Our amateur local effort involved the cooperation of an editor, graphic designer, six writers, seventeen photographers, and several dozen financial contributors."

One of the most interesting moments of the committee meetings occurred when Bob announced that he had asked Ron Polinder, the former Executive Director of Concerned Christian Citizens and, at that time, principal of Lynden Christian High School, to write one of the chapters for the book.

Members of the committee, tree-huggers all, were aghast. With all of the property rights claims coming from conservatives in the north part of the county, had Bob lost his mind? He reminded the committee of the latter part of the third goal for the book—to portray a diversity of points of view about the landscape. Though I'm certain all were not satisfied, the decision was accepted and we pushed on.

While Ron's chapter was not what any member of the committee would have written, it was clear to us, when we read it, that it was important it be included. In his chapter he recounts the formation of the Land Trust:

"This organization did not begin at Huxley College of Western Washington University, or as an offshoot of the Democratic Party, or the brainchild of an environmentalist from Fairhaven. The Whatcom Land Trust was conceived in the basement of Dutch Mothers Restaurant, downtown Lynden. In 1983, Concerned Christian Citizens, having an interest in farmland protection, was contacted by the Trust for Public Land. A forum in cooperation with TPL attracted fifty people, including County Councilman Bob Muencher, Trillium founder David Syre, attorney Rand Jack, stewards like Hilda Bajema, farmers like Herman Miller. Group chemistry insured more discussion; eventually the Whatcom County Land Trust was born."

In an unconventional ending of the chapter that takes the form of a long prayer, he writes:

"Father, I pray for my community, all my friends and fellow citizens, that we will do justice to the land, to the creatures, to all, I pray for an ethic that will move us to be stewards of the earth. I pray for a grateful heart to appreciate this wonderful place in Creation called Whatcom County and its smaller part called Lynden."

He had provided the obvious answer to those who said, "I'll do what I want with my land."

"It's not your land."

Ten thousand copies of the ninety-six-page pictorial were printed, and over the course of the next ten years we sold just over forty percent of those at Village Books.

As the book entered its ninth year and the print run neared exhaustion, the question arose of what to do with the book. The Land Trust could just congratulate itself and let it go. After all, nearly ten thousand copies of the book were in circulation and, though fundraising was not an original goal, the Land Trust had netted more than $150,000 from sales of the book—all of which had been put to use protecting land. Or they could reprint the book just as it was. Or a new, or partially new, book could be published.

After consultation with several of the original committee members, the third option was chosen, and a committee was reconvened, including several of the those original members. With more than sixty percent new photographs, a couple of new chapters, interviews with a dozen local residents, a new fold-out map of Land Trust properties, and a foreword by Pulitzer Prize-winning author Bill Dietrich, the book grew to 137 pages.

Whatcom Places II was published on November 15, and in six weeks became the Village Books number one bestseller for 2006. It came in at number four the next year, and though it's slipped down the list a bit since, continues to appear in our top books each year.

During the summer of 1998, Allison Smith of the British Booksellers Association called.

"Chuck, we'd like to bring you over to be part of a seminar for booksellers," she said. "Would you do that?"

"When is it?" I asked.

"It's on September 7th. We'd like to have you here a couple of days early to work with the other folks," she said.

"Gee, Allison, I'm sorry," I said. "Dee and I are taking a Rick Steves tour of Turkey. We fly through London on the 10th, and we already have our tickets."

"Well, what if we pay to change both of your tickets and put you up for a week in London? Could you do that?" she asked.

"Twist my other arm," I said.

Obviously, the deal was too good to pass. We went to London on the Friday before the seminar, met with the other participants on Saturday, and spent Sunday in the countryside with the group. After finishing the presentations on Monday, we had until Friday afternoon, when our plane left for Istanbul, to play in London.

The program came at a time when U.S. chain stores had begun to make advances into Great Britain. Borders had just opened in Oxford Circus, and booksellers in England were anxious to know how American booksellers had reacted to the roll out of big box chain stores. In addition to myself, the other presenters from the U.S. were Valerie Lewis of Hicklebee's in San Jose, Fred Hoffman of Wordsworth in Cambridge, and Richard Hunt of Bantam Doubleday Dell Publishing Company—the friend who had been with me on the USIA trip to Jordan and Morocco. We were joined by Irene Roele, a senior lecturer in strategic marketing at London Guildhall University.

Though some booksellers were anxiously preparing for the onslaught, others were in denial. Knowing how fast the big boxes spread in our country, I bet Tim Godfray, the Director of the British Booksellers Association, that by 2005 there would be twenty of the big chain stores there.

"Britain is different," said Tim. "I don't think that will happen here."

I'm still waiting to collect on my bet. At last count, though they are in receivership, Borders alone had more than thirty stores in the U.K., with five in London.

Dee and I don't consider ourselves tour bus travelers, so signing up for a tour of Turkey was a bit of a stretch. It was, however, a Rick Steves tour. We knew it would be atypical—only twenty-four people on a forty-eight passenger bus, no pay-as-you-go side trips, well-paid guides and bus drivers who don't depend on shopping kickbacks, and a close-to-the-ground itinerary that doesn't depend on Western-style hotels.

We arrived in Istanbul late Friday evening and were on our own to explore the city until Monday evening, when the tour group would gather for dinner and a brief orientation. Our hotel was built against one wall of Topkapi palace in the old city. We had learned which Istanbul sites we would not be visiting on the tour, including Dolmabahçe Palace, and spent our time exploring those.

The first two days of the tour were spent in Istanbul with tours of the Blue Mosque, the Hagia Sophia–the most magnificent of all Byzantine churches, now a museum, Topkapi Palace, the Chora Church, the Egyptian Spice Market and the new town. We capped off the second day with a cruise along the Bosphorus and dinner on the Asian side, before boarding an overnight train for Ankara.

In the capital city we visited the Anatolian Civilizations Museum and the Atatürk Mausoleum, the final resting place of the first President of Turkey—the man responsible for the reforms that created a secular Turkish government.

The thirteen-day tour included a couple of days in Cappadocia, a visit to the Mevlana Rumi Museum, sailing on the Mediterranean, and tours of Aphrodisias and Ephesus.

The highlights of the trip were eating lunch in a home in a small village, a visit with an Imam, and having tea with a nomadic family in their black tent. Though there were many other interesting and exciting encounters on the trip, these three were experiences we would not likely have been able to have on our own. Having our guide Lale as a translator made all three possible.

In each case we were able to hear, through Lale, the personal stories of Turkish life. The farming family in the small village who hosted us for lunch knew far more about the U.S. than any of us knew of Turkey. The Imam's life, looking after those in his village, was much like that of any minister, priest, or rabbi. The family in the black tent, though living a primitive, nomadic life, cared deeply about the education of their children.

The group we traveled with were interesting, fun, and, in all ways, great traveling companions. Except for one guy. From the beginning his behavior seemed a bit odd. He was constantly gathering people together for staged photos as if herding small children. He complained about accommodations and offered that he would gladly pay much more to be in better hotels. He objected to eating in the private home because he believed it unsanitary—it was as clean as any house we've lived in—and he refused tea at the black tent.

With one day left of the tour, as we were arriving in Kusadasi, Lale told us that the hotel we would be staying in might be noisy, with outdoor movies showing on one side and a disco just down the street. She reminded us of the earplugs we had been given and suggested this might be the night to break them out. Earplugs in place, Dee and I slept soundly through the night.

The next morning there was a swirl of conversation in the breakfast room. At ten o'clock the night before, Mr. Odd had stormed to Lale's room and bitterly complained about the tour. His tone and language had been extremely abusive. The tours always have someone from the office accompanying the group, and Mary Ann was on her first tour of duty in that capacity. Not sure of what to do, she called the office. Someone there, perhaps Rick himself, told her to remove him from the tour. She did.

He was doing his best to gain sympathy for his cause, but given his earlier behavior, was having an uphill battle. I think we all felt sorry for his wife—perhaps not just in this instance. She had been very nice and was, probably not for the first time, a victim of her husband's inappropriate behavior.

The group spent its last day visiting Ephesus with its Library of Celsus, which once held nearly 12,000 scrolls; the Basilica of St. John, built by Justinian I over the site of the apostle's tomb; and the single column that remains of the Temple of Artemis, one of the Seven Wonders of the Ancient World. We also visited the House of the Virgin nearby where, according to Christian tradition, Mary, mother of Jesus, spent her last days under the care of the Apostle John.

After a farewell dinner and a last evening in Kusadasi, most of us took the ferry to Samos, a Greek island just a few miles off the Turkish coast. We spent two nights there before Dee and I went by ferry to Santorini and then flew to Athens for our last three days before heading home.

Shortly after returning home, we received a copy of a letter Mr. Odd sent to Rick Steves reiterating his complaints and saying his entire trip had been based on going to Ephesus and that he couldn't do that after being kicked off the tour. Anyone who has been to Kusadasi knows that one would have to be deaf, blind and pretty stupid not to be able to get a dozen miles to Ephesus. He wanted his money back.

When I talked with Rick some time after our trip, he told me that they had refunded half of the cost of the entire tour. Though we both knew that Mr. Odd and his wife had received far more value than that, we agreed that it made good business sense to give the refund.

There's a belief that what we spend our lives doing can strongly influence what we become. Perhaps Mr. Odd was living proof of the theory. He was a proctologist.

The entire experience reminded me of something John Steinbeck wrote in *Travels With Charlie*:

I remember an old Arab in North Africa, a man whose hands had never felt water. He gave me mint tea in a glass so coated with use that it was opaque, but he handed me companionship, and the tea was wonderful because of it. And without any protection my teeth didn't fall out, nor did running sores develop. I began to formulate a new law describing the relationship of protection to despondency. A sad soul can kill you quicker, far quicker, than a germ.

In a personal sense, the decade didn't end well for us. When our friends and mentors, Norman and Patti, sold their bookstore in Oak Harbor, they moved to Bellingham and worked with us for nearly a year before taking a trip to Europe. They then opened Watermark Book Company in Anacortes.

A few years after opening Watermark, Norman collapsed while in France. He was diagnosed with cancer and began treatment. About a year later we jubilantly celebrated Norman's fiftieth birthday. He was apparently cancer-free. But the disease was persistent, and it showed up again.

On the way to the airport for a European vacation in September of 1999, Dee and I stopped to see Norman at Swedish Hospital. He had just been admitted and expected to be there only a short time. We didn't know it would be the last time we would see him. Less than a week after arriving in Europe, we learned that we'd lost our friend. We dedicated that winter's *Chuckanut Reader* to him this way:

Norman was one of the best booksellers we have ever known. He had a passion for books and for putting the right book in the hands of the right person. He and Patti were our first and lasting mentors in the business, beginning that role the day we met them twenty years ago. But beyond being a great bookseller, Norman was a great person. He was funny, smart, kind, and generous, and someone who just made you feel good to be with. We miss him dearly and so does the world of books.

Chapter 7

A New Home
2000–2004

I was sitting in a hotel bar in Tarrytown, NY, talking with Mike Powell of Powell's Books in Portland. We had been friends since serving together many years earlier on the PNBA board. Later we shared time on the ABA board and were currently on the board of the American Booksellers Foundation for Free Expression. After ABFFE meetings that day, we were just winding down and swapping bookselling stories.

"Do you still have that bookmobile?" I asked.

"Yes," he said. "But I'll make you a deal on it."

"Don't you use it anymore?"

"Not really. We used to load it up and take it out to some of the corporate headquarters, but we don't do that anymore."

"How much do you want for it?"

Mike named a price and must have seen the interest in my eyes. "Come down and see it," he said.

Patrick Lorang had worked at the store for several years, but was at that time driving the bookmobile for the Whatcom County Library. He had been a busaholic for years. He'd owned a couple of buses, including one reputed to have belonged to Howard Hughes, and lusted after many others. I knew he would jump at the chance to go to Portland and check out the bookmobile for us. He did.

"If it checks out," I said, "drive it home."

Patrick just smiled and booked the train to Portland. In a couple of days our bookmobile was making its way up I-5.

After we stripped off the Powell's lettering, Lanny Little painted a mural of books on each side and, on the back, a portrait of Dee and me, holding a sign with this poem:

"Worthy friends, my wain doth hold
Many a book, both new and old;
Books, the truest friends of man,
Fill this rolling caravan.

Books to satisfy all uses,
Golden lyrics of the Muses,
Books on cookery and farming,
Novels passionate and charming,
Every kind for every need
So that he who buys may read."

The verse is taken from Christopher Morley's book *Parnassus on Wheels*, the story of one bookseller buying a rolling bookstore—in that case a horse-drawn wagon—from another bookseller. Now we had an odd case of life imitating fiction.

On July 8, 2000, the day the 4th Harry Potter book was released, the bookmobile made its first public appearance at the Bellingham Farmers Market, loaded with books and draped with a banner saying "Harry is Here." A regular schedule for our own parnassus on wheels included supermarket parking lots in Ferndale, Everson, and Bellingham, and a regular Sunday afternoon appearance near Pastazza in Barkley Village. It also became a welcome oasis for book lovers at the Northwest Washington Fair for four years, and made appearances at Bookfest in Seattle, holiday fairs, and other events around Whatcom County.

Though generally in pretty good running order, the vehicle did present us with a couple of mechanical challenges. The first year at the fair, we had not put an electrical switch in the correct position, realizing only when we were ready to drive off that we had drained the battery. But the most interesting mechanical failure occurred one afternoon when Robert Gruen returned from Everson. He walked into the store looking quite shaken.

"What's wrong?" I asked.

"The brakes failed on the bookmobile."

"Where?"

"I was going through the light on Mount Baker Highway, near Sunset Square, and couldn't stop."

"Where did you leave the bookmobile?

"It's up on 12th Street, near the laundromat."

I would have left it on the side of the road and walked back if need be, but Robert had nursed it clear across town without brakes. Fortunately, he knew better than to head down the hill to its regular parking spot where the new building is now located. We had it towed and fixed, and we all agreed to be extremely careful when driving it and not to keep driving if the brakes failed again.

Minor mechanical problems became more frequent, and we joked that we should have Jasmine Valandani, one of the most frequent drivers of the bookmobile, call "Car Talk" about its ills. We thought the Tappet brothers would appreciate a woman with an unusual voice calling about a bookmobile that was built in 1967. But, between its ailments and our failure to generate any serious business with it, we retired our rolling bookstore before Jasmine had a chance to have fun with them. The "wain" became a billboard on wheels at the corner of Old Fairhaven Parkway and 30th Street until we let it go in May, 2010.

Barbara Kingsolver had a much larger crowd than before when she returned to Bellingham for her book *Prodigal Summer*. She had agreed with the publisher to do only five events in the entire country, which would be decided by judging proposals from bookstores. The proposed event had to be held off-site from the bookstore, with a reasonable ticket price that would benefit an environmental organization.

Because of the great popularity Barbara had garnered with her bestselling book *The Poisonwood Bible*, the publisher was inundated with proposals, which they were able to reduce to nine finalists before reaching a point of indecision. They passed the nine proposals to Barbara and asked her to make the choices. Impressed by the quality of the requests and the work being done by the environmental groups that would benefit, she decided she would do all nine events. Village Books was one of those nine, and North Cascades Institute was the beneficiary of that evening's event—to the tune of $9000.

The crowd of more than twelve hundred was wowed as Barbara not only spoke about and read from her book, but talked about each of the environmental programs benefitting from her tour. It was clear that her heart was in it. Personally it was a great night for us as well. After Barbara signed hundreds of books for folks, we slipped off to sip wine and chat with her and her husband Steven at the home of NCI Executive Director Saul Weisberg and his wife Shelley.

Over the years Rick Steves has become a friend, and Village Books brings him to town for a yearly event, usually in one of the larger school auditoriums where he draws up to eight hundred people. On those occasions he presents a full three-hour travel seminar, complete with inspirational slides of various "back doors" as well as a wealth of travel tips.

In December of 2000, after working until closing the night before, Dee and I left for Paris on Christmas morning. We had rented an apartment in the 15th arrondissement and were staying for two weeks. Instead of just vacationing, we were living like locals. Each morning we would go down to the local patisserie to get a baguette and croissants. We shopped in the local grocery and spent quite a bit of time exploring the neighbor-hood, which was not a tourist destination.

Early one evening as we left the Pompidou Centre, we noticed a familiar couple walking toward us—Rick and Anne Steves. They were as surprised to see us as we were to see them. We stopped and chatted on the street and then continued on our way.

Late in January, following that trip, Rick arrived for his yearly presentation with us in Bellingham, and we were talking about having met on the street in Paris.

"We were about three blocks down the street," Rick said, "when Anne turned to me and said, 'why didn't we all go to dinner together?'"

"Dee said the same thing," I responded.

We had been heading for a restaurant that Rick had recommended in his latest Paris book, and they were going to try a new restaurant. What fun it would have been to be part of that sampling process. Had we met on the street in Seattle, that likely would have happened, but the surprise of bumping into one another that far from home just knocked the sense out of us.

The largest undertaking, and I use the word advisedly, in which we have ever engaged was the planning and construction of our new bookstore building. Anyone who has ever been involved in a building project knows that one loses total control of timelines and costs. Such projects also come to dominate nearly every waking thought, in this case, over several years.

In the Summer 2001 edition of the *Chuckanut Reader* we proudly announced our plans for the new building. Under the headline "2001, A 'New Space' Odyssey," we said, "Now that we're turning 21, we thought it might be time to move into our own place. So we've begun the design phase of a new building on the corner of Eleventh Street and Mill Avenue, just north of

Paper Dreams (or, for the visual, the spot where we've parked the Bookmobile for the last year or so)."

The article went on to talk about our expected time frame: "Barring major problems (or, as Tennessee Ernie Ford used to say, 'God willin' and the creeks don't rise') we will break ground next January and be in the new space by fall of 2002."

That story also outlined some of the expected changes in the store—an elevator, better natural and artificial lighting, more seating, better access to shelves, climate control, and nicer restrooms. We also asked two questions of our customers to help us in the planning process: 1) What do you see as the defining physical features of Village Books that we should make every attempt to maintain? and 2) What would you like to have in the new store that is currently lacking?

In addition to soliciting responses by email, we also had forms that folks could pick up at the counters. We had many responses to our questions. A lot of them confirmed the features we had been planning for the store. Others asked for expansion of particular sections. One of the most interesting patterns emerged in answer to question number one. People said they wanted us to retain the wooden floors and brick walls. That was absolutely fine with us, except...the old store did not have wooden floors and brick walls.

Well, that's not entirely accurate. The Colophon Café had a wooden floor in the upper level and a brick wall behind that counter. There was also a stone wall in the café on the lower level and brick pillars between the café and bookstore on that floor. Aside from that, all bookstore floors were carpeted and the walls were painted wallboard.

So, were folks just delusional? No. Our architect, Dave Christensen, explained it to us: "It's not uncommon for architects to include smaller sections of some materials to influence people's perceptions of the entire space," he said. "Take a bank, for example. Rather than use marble flooring throughout the space, at great expense, we might create a marble entrance area instead. Many people will remember the floor as being marble."

Thus, folks perceived the old location of the bookstore as having wooden floors and brick walls. We could have just laughed it off, but we realized folks were implying something far more important in what they asked for. There was a warm feeling conveyed by those materials that they associated with the atmosphere of the store. We planned the new space with wooden floors on two levels and a long brick wall on the main floor. We also planned an open ceiling above much of the main floor to avoid a "slick" look in the store.

As you may know, the new space did not open in fall 2002. There were several issues that caused delays. The first came after submitting our plans for preliminary approval. The zoning for the block in which the building is located allows building to a height of fifty-four feet, with no variance needed if some public amenities are included. We had held a voluntary meeting with neighbors to explain our building project and hear concerns. There were some questions about whether views from Judson Plaza, immediately across Eleventh Street, would be blocked.

After visiting the roof decks—the only area from which most of the Judson Plaza condos had a westerly view—we decided to lower the building, even though it would be at greater cost because floors between the new building and the existing Paper Dreams building would not be at the same level. We submitted the plans to the City. The plans were approved with a further agreement that we would never build higher on the Paper Dreams building. We thought we were on our way.

A short time after approval we learned that the residents of Judson Plaza had filed suit to stop the building being built at the approved height. In November of 2001 a hearing date was set, but it wouldn't be until March 19 of 2002. After months of waiting and a very short hearing, the judge upheld the approval to build, and we thought we were now on the fast track.

Financing, however, proved to be our next stumbling block.

We were creating a mixed-use building with both retail and residential components, the type of building encouraged in urban villages. The Small Business Administration immediately agreed to guarantee financing for the retail portion of the building. However, we had planned two condominiums—including our own home—for the top floor of the building, and SBA is precluded by law from financing residential projects. That meant securing mixed financing.

But no comparable condominiums had been sold in the area, so it was difficult to get a realistic appraisal. Because of the lower appraisal of the condos, the cost of constructing the building was out of line with its assumed value. We had a great team at a local bank doing everything that they could to make the financing work, but once they approved it here, it had to go to Bellevue for final approval. The Bellevue office denied it. The local bank folks were so upset that one of them offered to help us get financing through another local bank.

We were in the process of working on that when David Ebenal walked into the bookstore one day, introduced himself, and said, "I understand your financing is stalled."

"That's right," I said.

"Well, I'd like to buy your lot."

"We're going to build a new bookstore there," I said. "We don't want to sell the lot."

"Then let me build the new building."

I explained that we had gone through a rigorous process of interviewing several builders and had chosen a builder we thought we'd be very happy with.

"At least sit down and talk to me about it," he urged.

We set a date, and over the course of several meetings we were able to come to a greater understanding of what each of us wanted from the project. Dee and I had been convinced that we wanted to own our building. Then one day I said to Dee, "You know, owning a building is just a strategy. What is it we really want?"

"We want to be able to design the space for the store," she said.

"We've pretty much done that already, haven't we?"

"Yes, but we also want to live above the store and not have rising occupancy costs for the store drive us out of business," she said.

"Suppose we could do all of those things without owning the building."

"Do you think we could?"

I had no idea whether we could manage that, but we began talking with David Ebenal. Once it became clear that we were interested in having both parties get what they needed, the negotiations kicked into high gear. Dave agreed to buy the Paper Dreams building and the lot next to it. He also agreed to buy the plans that we had developed with Dave Christensen and to construct the new building to those specifications.

What we got in return was some money, the mortgage-free condo we had designed for ourselves above the store, and a long term lease on all the commercial space in the new building and the Paper Dreams building, which were now legally combined into one building.

It was the lease that was the most unusual part of the agreement. Many commercial leases have some kind of rent escalators built in and very little protection from rent hikes at the time of renewal. Most of the good bookstores that have closed over the past few years had been seriously impacted by rising rents. We agreed to a ten-year lease with two five-year options, and that the rental costs would be determined by the cost of Ebenal's building loans at each five-year renewal, based on a predetermined index. That rental rate would then lock in until the next renewal. Each of our attorneys agreed that this was the most creative lease arrangement they had ever worked on.

We were thrilled, but it would still be some time before we moved into the new building.

One of the truly moving events we've been part of at the store happened when David James Duncan came to read from *My Story as Told by Water*. John Marshall wrote the following in the October 5, 2001, *Seattle Post Intelligencer*. It appears here with permission.

"Book Brings an Author, Grieving Mom Together"

by John Marshall

A writer wants nothing more than readers, the ultimate reward for all the solitary work with words. But readers' reactions also can surprise writers, as David James Duncan has found. The Montana author has penned such powerful novels as *The Brothers K* and *The River Why*, but was unprepared for what keeps happening with readers. "One of the really poignant and difficult things has been that I keep meeting parents who have lost children, children who read and loved my books," Duncan said. "These parents want some connection to something their lost child loved. This has happened to me dozens of times." It happened again recently when Duncan went to Bellingham to read from his fine new collection of essays, *My Story as Told by Water* (Sierra Club Books). The book includes a remarkable passage dedicated to Liam Wood, an 18-year-old from Bellingham who was fly-fishing in Whatcom Creek when it was engulfed in a 1999 conflagration from a gas leak in the Olympic Pipe Line. News stories after Wood's death pointed out that he was a great fan of Duncan's writing, especially *The River Why*, and word of that soon got back to the writer himself. It was something that Duncan, a passionate and intuitive fellow, did not forget.

So when Duncan went to Bellingham, he made a pilgrimage to the site of Wood's passing. The creek area was still scorched, but Duncan picked up blackened rocks in the water and found teeming life. Duncan showed similar resolve when he was told the Village Books audience included Marlene Robinson and Bruce Brabec, Wood's mother and stepfather.

The standing-room crowd of 150 was spellbound as Duncan cast aside his new book and instead read "The Mickey Mantle Koan" from *River Teeth*, an elegiac account of the death of his older brother, another young man who never got to see the age of 19. There were times when it seemed the 49-year-old Duncan might be too overcome with emotion to continue, but he pressed on.

"I just wanted Liam's mother to know," Duncan said later, "that if my fly-fishing character was a hero to him, then he was also a hero to me."

Robinson sat transfixed in the public event turned so personal.

"As hard as it was to sit in a hot and crowded room and have such an intimate thing occur," Robinson recalled, "what David Duncan did gave back something important to me. He expressed his own courage in choosing to read that amazingly eloquent story. Every day, I have to find a reason and a way to keep going. David's reading was a real gift to me in that way, since he was able to be so courageous and so vulnerable."

The mother and the writer met briefly after the reading, a few hurried moments, but meaningful to them both. Robinson was heartened that this stranger, who had been a hero to her late son, who had inspired his passion for fly-fishing and later writing as well, had proved to be the "kindred spirit" and "worthy role model" that she had expected.

Duncan was heartened that reaching out and confronting grief in public, however painful, seemed appropriate.

"I know that just talking doesn't help that much with grief

of that size, but what else do we have to offer? We need to walk with them."

Duncan's reading in Bellingham had another benefit. The $5 admission, boosted by a contribution from Village Books, raised $1000 for the Nooksack Salmon Enhancement Association, which has devoted years to restoring lower Whatcom Creek even before the firestorm upstream.

Every Thursday, Robinson takes a day off from work and joins the volunteers restoring the stream where her son died. Others might shy away from such a weekly encounter, but not this woman, who explains why she does this and sounds much like a character in a Duncan novel, or even like Duncan himself.

"There is something heart-wrenching about going to Whatcom Creek," Robinson said. "I never forget what happened, 24 hours a day, whether I'm sleeping or dreaming. I know that Liam is gone, but I would rather be engaged in it. And I love being in nature—that's the one place where I feel some peace and calm."

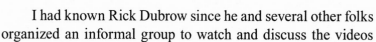

I had known Rick Dubrow since he and several other folks organized an informal group to watch and discuss the videos from Paul Hawken's PBS show, "Growing a Business." We knew that we shared many values about business, the environment, and community.

He came to see me one day in 2001 to pick my brain about a group he wanted to get restarted. He and a handful of friends, mostly in the building trades, had formed an environmental business group about four years earlier, but as they had each become involved in other projects, the organization had become dormant.

After trading ideas, Rick asked if I would join a steering committee. He also told me about a couple—Michelle and

Derek Long—who had just moved to the area and wanted to work with the group. The committee, including the Longs, began meeting, and with the help of an organizational facilitator formed a board of directors.

Thus was born—or, more accurately, reborn—Sustainable Connections. Its vision captures what the organization is about: "We envision a thriving, collaborative community in which local businesses are prosperous and contribute to a healthy environment and the well-being of all citizens."

SC signed up its first business member in April of 2003, and because of its successes in green building, sustainable agriculture, renewable energy, and supporting independent local businesses, it has grown to more than 650 member businesses. Its most visible—and most copied—program is "Think Local First."

One of the ideas Rick and I had talked about at that first meeting was encouraging the support of local businesses. Now I had the opportunity to help establish a program here to accomplish that.

Like many other programs Sustainable Connections has launched, "Think Local First" has been wildly successful. In fact, an independent research firm learned that 69% of Bellingham residents were familiar with the program. A business measuring the effectiveness of a marketing program would be ecstatic with 10 or 15% awareness. More important, three out of five people surveyed said they had changed their behavior based on information they had learned from the program.

Among the most convincing information about buying local are the results of studies, replicated around the country, that show that locally owned, independent businesses generate much greater economic impact—sometimes three times more—than corporate stores. Local stores usually have higher local payrolls because they don't source services outside of the community, they spend locally for goods, and they retain and invest a larger share of their profits locally.

Similarly persuasive facts: small, local businesses contribute

250% more to non-profits than large businesses; local businesses help reduce environmental impacts; and they also keep communities from all looking and feeling exactly the same.

My work with Sustainable Connections' "Think Local First" program inspired me to write this article for our Summer 2004 *Chuckanut Reader*:

I grew up in rural Illinois surrounded by fields of corn and soy beans and…coal mines. Unlike Whatcom County's coal mines that left subterranean tunnels under parts of the county (including downtown Bellingham), these were strip mines that left deep, often water-filled pits and piles of soil and rock. Strip mining destroyed acres and acres of productive farmland and left in its wake large areas of unusable land. What I witnessed as a child was captured in song by John Prine when he wrote "Paradise." Though writing about Kentucky, the words could well be applied to the place of my childhood as well:

> *And Daddy won't you take me back to Muhlenberg county,*
>
> *Down by the Green River, where Paradise lay.*
>
> *"Well I'm sorry, my son, but you're too late in askin'.*
>
> *Mr. Peabody's coal train has hauled it away."*

Though the days of that kind of strip mining have passed, many of the scars on the land remain. While there's no doubt the coal was needed—I grew up in a coal-heated house—its method of extraction and the absence of land restoration certainly were a high (and hidden) cost to pay for it.

Whatcom County is no longer a source of coal but, in my opinion, the shaft mines of old have been replaced by a modern form of strip mining. That strip mining takes the form of out-of-state, corporate retail companies building their big-box stores to extract, not coal, but dollars from the local economy.

Of course we need (or, at least, want) many of the goods the big boxes sell. But, at what (hidden) cost? Are we willing to sacrifice local businesses that contribute more dollars to the local economy and fund non-profit organizations at a much greater level than non-local, corporate companies? Are we willing to have empty big-boxes dotting the landscape when one national company decides to take market share away from another? Are we willing to give up the civic involvement that locals engage in? There are certainly hidden costs to the retail strip mining that is rolling across Whatcom County. And we can make choices that avoid those costs and negative consequences.

I hope that this generation's children and grandchildren will never have the occasion to sing (with apologies to John Prine) these words to Paradise:

> *And Daddy won't you take me back to ol' Whatcom County,*
>
> *Down by the Nooksack, where Paradise lay.*
>
> *"Well I'm sorry, my son, but you're too late in askin'.*
>
> *Big Retail's cash train has hauled it away."*

Village Books became, and remains, a sustaining member of Sustainable Connections. I served on the board for five years and continue to be involved with what I believe is one of the most effective community organizations that exists.

Four plainclothes Denver police arrived at the Tattered Cover bookshop one day in March of 2001, with a search warrant, demanding to know if a particular drug book had been purchased there and, if so, by whom. Owner Joyce Meskis refused to give them any information, and was able to get her attorney Dan Recht on the phone. He convinced the police to leave without enforcing the warrant.

He was then able to get a hearing to quash the warrant, something that often happens with subpoenas, but not search warrants. I was flown to Denver to be an "expert witness" in that hearing. In spite of arguments by Recht that the police had failed to interview witnesses and that there were less obtrusive ways of gathering evidence, the judge ruled against the Tattered Cover.

Joyce now had to decide whether to appeal to the Colorado Supreme Court, and after careful deliberation, decided to do so. On April 8, 2002, the court ruled unanimously that the government failed to show a compelling need for the records. More importantly, the court held that "in the future, anytime the government seeks to obtain such records, the bookstore must be afforded a due-process hearing in advance, where a court will determine whether law enforcement officials have a sufficiently compelling need for the information."

A similar privacy issue had been raised when Special Prosecutor Kenneth Starr demanded to see Monica Lewinsky's purchase records from two D.C. bookshops. In that case, Lewinsky struck a deal with Starr and the case never moved to court.

The American Booksellers Foundation for Free Expression was deeply involved in both of these cases. ABFFE also worked (and continues to work) with bookstores and libraries around privacy concerns caused by the PATRIOT Act.

One of those privacy concerns occurred right here in Whatcom County. On June 8, 2004, an FBI agent demanded from the Deming library branch the names of all patrons who had borrowed *Bin Laden: The Man Who Declared War on America*. A reader, apparently thinking it a threat, had reported to the FBI a handwritten note in the book's margin: "If the things I'm doing is considered a crime then let history be a witness that I am a criminal. Hostility toward America is a religious duty and we hope to be rewarded by God."

The library, under the leadership of Library Director Joan Airoldi, refused to hand over information unless served with a subpoena, and the Library Board voted to fight any orders that might be issued. A grand jury subpoena was issued and the board voted to file a motion to quash it. The FBI later withdrew the subpoena.

Joan Airoldi was awarded the PEN/Newman's Own First Amendment Award at a Gala in New York City in June of 2005. Speaking about the award and the incident that prompted it, PEN Freedom to Write Program Director Larry Siems said, "What Joan Airoldi and her staff and Board did—standing up to an unwarranted intrusion by federal agents into the privacy of ordinary Americans—was heroic in itself. At the same time, their success vividly illustrates why the protections states and courts have carved out for reading records are so essential."

Siems went on to say, "If the FBI had returned not with a Grand Jury subpoena but with a PATRIOT Act order, the library would have been unable to challenge the request in court, and the reading records of law-abiding patrons may well have made their way into FBI files."

In the spring of 2001, while driving across town with my friend Bob Keller, I pointed out Mount Baker, bathed in sunlight. "I really have no interest in mountaineering," I said. "But, having looked at that mountain for more than twenty years, I'd love to stand on top of it some day."

Bob recalled the lure of Mount Rainier when he was a boy growing up in Tacoma. "I can understand that," he said.

The next day, while I was away from the store, Bob stopped in and talked with Dee. "Would you pass a message on to Chuck, even if you don't like it?"

"Sure. What's the message?"

"Tell him I'll take him up Baker. I can't do it this year, but we'll go next summer."

The next spring we began training for the climb. On our first day, Bob took me to the Pine and Cedar Lakes Trail, just south of town. I was not in good condition, and even with a very light pack, wondered after just ten minutes if I would ever take another full breath in my life.

The next week on that trail was better. Then we did Oyster Dome and regularly plodded up and down Taylor Street from the Chrysalis to the top, then up and down the stairs a few times before heading down toward the bay, each week with increasingly heavier packs.

We did some hiking in snow out in the foothills, and as the climb drew nearer, practiced self-arrests with ice axes. Bob, in typical ex-professorial style, recommended some reading. *Mountaineering: The Freedom of the Hills* by Graydon and Hanson had first been published in 1960 and was in its sixth edition, and my reading about snow, ice, and alpine climbing gave me some preparation for what I was going to face.

On July 11th, seven of us began our trek up Heliotrope Ridge to set up base camp at the edge of the Coleman Glacier, at about 5500 feet—2000 feet above the trailhead, but nearly 5300 feet below our goal. In preparation for the outing I had rented a subzero sleeping bag for its warmth and light weight, but the temperature at base camp didn't drop below fifty degrees, and I spent most of the night on top of the bag.

Of the other six members of our excursion, four had considerable climbing experience—one had summitted Baker 28 times. The other novice was a twenty-something fireman and EMT. As a friend noted before the climb, I was the weak link.

Just before three the next morning, after roping up in three teams, we began our ascent. A relatively late start, soft snow, two novices, and one dehydrated climber with leg cramps conspired to slow our journey upward. It was nearly noon when we reached the peak, where we lunched and took pictures—we could see all the way to Mt. Rainier—before beginning our descent.

The warmth of the day allowed for t-shirts, but also caused us to sink into the snow—sometimes to mid-thigh, slowing and tiring us. Still, we made it to base camp and began to pack up. I've been unmercifully teased about what happened there.

I rolled the rented sleeping bag and set it to the side while we packed other items and struck tents.

"Hey, Chuck," Bob shouted. "Look!"

I spun around to see the sleeping bag rolling down the slope. It was far enough away and the terrain so steep that it wouldn't have been wise to chase it. I just had to hope it would hit something and stop. Soon everyone was gathered around watching the sleeping bag pick up momentum. There was a slight upward slope just before a sheer drop. My only hope was that it would slow and stop before the edge.

As it reached the brink it appeared to catch on the rim and come to a halt. Then, just as we all breathed a sigh of relief, and I prepared to pick my way down to the bag, it teetered and fell over the edge. Thinking I may still be able to retrieve it, I carefully descended to the rim and looked over. The bag was nowhere in sight, and there was no way to get down into the deep ravine. It was clear that I was going to have to buy the bag, and I'd never even needed it. At least my gear would be lighter hiking out.

I had never fully understood the legendary mountaineer's answer to the question of why he climbed a mountain. Now, totally exhausted but with spirits elevated, I surely did—"Because it's there."

Every national convention we've attended has been exciting in one way or another, and the 2002 BEA in New York City was no exception. It had been eleven years since our convention and tradeshow had set foot in the Big Apple, a bit ironic since it is the center of U.S. publishing.

As always, there were numerous author events, seminars, and parties, which were educational, inspiring, and just plain fun. Among them, two events that year really stand out—being at the "Rosie O'Donnell Show" to see a Bellingham author interviewed, and spending some time with Michael Moore.

It was serendipitous that Clara Kelly, author of *The Flamboya Tree*, was booked to tape a national TV show at the same time we were meeting in NYC. Clara, who calls Dee and me the "God Parents" of her memoir (simply for guiding her to Sara Stamey, who in turn helped her get it published), insisted we take two tickets and attend the show.

Rosie was obviously touched by the book—a memoir of spending four years in a Japanese concentration camp—and Clara did a great job of answering questions and talking about her amazing experience. We were really glad we were there.

Having secured the privilege in an auction conducted by the American Booksellers Foundation for Free Expression, Paul Haskins, Dee, and I went to spend a couple of hours with Michael Moore, first watching him doing final sound editing on his film *Bowling for Columbine*, then chatting about topics from publishing and bookselling to national politics. He told us we were the first "civilians" to see any part of the new film, which went on to win both the Cannes Prix Educational National Award and the Cannes 55th Anniversary Special Prize.

There was actually a third exciting event that no Northwesterner should fail to mention. We watched the Mariners beat the Yankees in the "house that Ruth built."

Early each January, when the holiday rush is behind us, the staff gathers for a party to celebrate the season and enjoy each other's company. At the 2004 party, Dee and I were presented with a very special gift. As I opened the present I realized I was staring at the bared gluteus maximi of Chad Helder and his partner, Tshombe. The calendar we'd been given was titled "The Staff of Village Books UNBOUND." Inspired by the Ladies of Rylstone, each staff member was photographed in a work-related setting... without clothes, carefully posed to avoid full exposure.

It was funny, but it was also very touching. Parents know the feeling of appreciating a child's homemade card far more than one from the store. It was the personal engagement in creating the gift that wowed us.

We later heard stories of the making of the calendar—staff coming into the store late at night to stage scenes and take pictures and enlisting photographic help from spouses. It had been quite a production.

We realized that acknowledgement of this unique gift required more than a store-bought thank you. So Dee and I posed, using the calendar itself to preserve modesty, and created our own thank you card to post in the staff lounge.

With the exception of JoAnn Hanesworth, who has managed our Paper Dreams store since its birth in 1982, Krista Hunter holds the record for length of employment. She joined us in the summer of of 1983 and was with us until August of 2007—more than twenty-four years. No individual has had a more significant, or longer lasting, impact on Village Books than Krista. She quickly took on responsibilities as a buyer for the store and led our buying team for many years.

More than one publishing company tried to lure her away to represent their books to bookstores. Fortunately for us, she liked it here and didn't want to be constantly on the road. She was considered by many in publishing to be one of the best book buyers in the country. She was also one of the most respected booksellers who has ever worked here. Everyone looked to her for advice, and she really set much of the tone in the store.

We had begun a tradition, when JoAnn completed her twentieth year managing Paper Dreams, of celebrating those landmarks by sending the person on a special trip—somewhere they had long been longing to see. JoAnn went to Hawaii, and we knew that Krista had a deep desire to go to the Galapagos Islands. Writing about her trip in the Spring 2004 edition of the *Chuckanut Reader* Krista said this:

One day as I worked the upstairs counter, Chuck came to me and asked quite nonchalantly if I would like to go to the Galapagos Islands. Of course I quickly said yes, thinking this was merely a rhetorical question—I had been telling Chuck and Dee both for years of my desire to visit the islands. Imagine how surprised I was when I realized this was not a question but an offer. As a gift for celebrating twenty years of working with Chuck and Dee and all the other great people at Village Books, I was given this trip to the Galapagos Islands. My joy and gratitude is unbounded. This truly was a trip of a lifetime, and the memories will keep me company for the rest of my life. Gracias!"

Each issue of The *Chuckanut Reader* includes a couple dozen previews of books that have just arrived or will be published over the next few months. These are usually grouped by category—fiction, biography, cooking, etc. In the spring of 2004 we grouped ten books in a two-page spread entitled "Politically Reading."

Nothing in our publication has ever elicited such a vocal response.

Mea Culpa by Chuck Robinson

The "Politically Reading" pages in our Summer *Chuckanut Reader* caused a bit of a stir. We received several—eight, I believe (which likely represent a considerably larger number of the same opinion)—phone calls and emails complaining about the lack of balance on the pages (coupled in at least two of the calls with a complaint about our reprinting of Margaret Atwood's opinion piece). The contacts took a few different forms. Some folks wanted us to know that they wouldn't be shopping at Village Books any longer because of the books we featured in the *Reader*. With our record of advocacy for free expression, you might imagine how we react to such threats. Some suggested in their complaints that we didn't carry books of other political opinions. One person even made a list of authors whom she asserted we didn't stock—we carry almost all of them. Most missed the fact that P.J. O'Rourke is a conservative in asserting all were of one political stripe (though that certainly doesn't mean there was a balance). Others were making a plea for some balance in letting them know what was available—a reasonable request, I must add. But the email that really hit me between the eyes was one from a person whom I greatly respect and admire and consider a friend. Though he is, on many issues, considerably more conservative than I—and perhaps most of us at Village Books—he is also extremely community-minded, thoughtful, articulate, and fiercely independent. He said he was beginning "to feel unwanted" in our bookstore. When I read that I realized that we had accomplished something we never intended. While many of us at the store have strongly held opinions about many subjects, we also value free expression and lively debate. The last thing we want to do is to close off conversation about important issues. In fact, our mission is to "connect people with the information and entertainment they seek—mostly in book form." So, while I will NEVER apologize for voicing my opinion—and will defend to the death your right to do the same, I certainly apologize (again) to my friend and to anyone who felt, because of the lack of balance, unwanted in our store.

As a practical matter it is important to make a distinction

between book previews, which are primarily promotional information from the publishers (the books on the "Politically Reading" pages were mostly previews), and book reviews, which are "signed" with the name of a staff person at Village Books or guest reviewer. Our selection of books to preview is based on what we expect our readers are most interested in. For example, politically speaking, we usually sell about six or seven times the number of Michael Moore books than we do Bill O'Reilly titles. Books that we review are those we ourselves have chosen to read and offer an opinion on. Book previews do not necessarily reflect our own opinions. Book reviews reflect the opinion of the individual reviewer, which may or may not be the view of others at Village Books. We do value free expression. We carry books reflecting many opinions. And, I do apologize once again for making anyone uncomfortable in Village Books.

The Fairhaven Village Green has become such a central piece of the neighborhood that it seems that it's always been there. For years, however, the back windows of the bookstore looked out over a weed-covered field that sloped down toward Tenth Street. The area was used in the '80s for the Fairhaven salmon barbecues and continued to be used for "It All Ends in Fairhaven" at the end of the Ski-to-Sea race.

When the property was acquired by the City with "Beyond Greenways" funds, the parks department convened a neighborhood group to plan its development. It was made clear from the beginning that funds did not exist for the park and that there would likely need to be a significant private contribution to the effort.

The group, composed of residents, business folks, and park staff, did its best to design an urban oasis that fit the district.

What was imagined was a Victorian-style pocket park with meandering paths, flower gardens, and a gazebo in the northwest corner with restrooms below it.

As expected, the plans were shelved, awaiting a time when dollars could be raised to move forward. In the meantime, various activities began to take place there. A large white projection screen was painted on the building in 1998 for the Whatcom Film Association (now the Pickford Film Center) to show films on summer evenings, and the farmers' market had moved its tents to the field. Two years later, Lanny Little painted a mural on the wall, framing the movie screen.

The increased activity in the area prompted one area business person to approach me. "I think we should try to get the gazebo built. We especially need public restrooms," she said.

I agreed and asked what she had in mind.

"We need to find some civic-minded person who could head up the project. Can you think of anyone?"

"What about Brian Griffin? He likes Fairhaven, and he's good at fundraising and getting projects moving."

"Brian's pretty busy. Maybe we should find someone who's retired and has nothing to do," she replied.

"That's not the way the world works, Denise. We need to get a busy person who really loves the project, and he or she will figure out a way to get it done. I'll call Brian."

A few days later, Brian and I met at the Colophon Café. I laid out our plans for the gazebo with restrooms and asked Brian, "Well, what do you think?"

"I can't get really excited about building Johns," he said. "But if this was about doing the whole park, that's another matter."

Brian had come to love the public spaces he saw throughout Europe and thought money could be raised to create that kind of place here, so he set about forming a committee—immediately asking me to serve—and working with Leslie Bryson at the parks department. Others on the committee included Denise Dibb-Thompson, Barbara and Howard Evans, J.C. Hickman,

Charles Onion, and Kate Weisel. We met regularly over the next several months and raised funds by selling bricks, benches, bowler hats, and paver stones.

With the changes in the uses of the area, it became clear that the existing plan for the park was not appropriate. Brian engaged architect John Stewart and worked with him to create a new plan. John, along with engineers, builders, and others, donated much or all of the work.

The cost of the park had been estimated at around half a million dollars. Brian had crafted a partnership with the City and guaranteed that the committee would raise $150,000. The costs for the park escalated to over a million dollars. Undaunted, the committee stepped up, and between fundraising and arranging pro bono work agreements, paid for about half of the final cost of the Fairhaven Village Green.

Brian was tireless in seeking out the proper materials for the project. Much of the lumber for the pergola was salvaged from a pier in Seattle, and he found granite for the bases of the pergola posts. He also designed the artistic manhole covers for the drainage system and the decorative metal posts that border the Green, and solicited Herb Ershig to design and build the metal gate for the under-stage restrooms. An old water fountain, once in downtown Bellingham, was procured, and he created the popular dog fountain.

Brian also spearheaded a design contest to select an artist to create a sculpture of the area's founder, Dirty Dan Harris. Robert McDermott won that commission and created the bench sculpture that now adorns the park. Hardly a day goes by that folks aren't spotted having their pictures taken, sitting next to Dan on the bench.

The pergola was erected by a group of volunteers in what resembled an old-fashioned barn raising. When Mark Asmundson, Mayor of Bellingham at the time, showed up that morning, some thought it was for a photo op. Mark, however, worked side by side with the rest of the volunteers, all day long. By the end of the day it was obvious to most folks that he was among the most valuable workers.

There was music, storytelling, and a variety of kids' activities when the Fairhaven Village Green was dedicated on April 26, 2003. And the Fairhaven Middle School Band led a Dirty Dan portrayer to the Green, where he unveiled the sculpture of his namesake before the Mayor dedicated the park.

When the project was completed, Brian Griffin, without whom it never would have happened, said, "Everything I've done civically in my life has led to doing this project." To hear Brian (and his wife Marya) talk, this would be the last big project that he would ever take on. A short time later he and his friend Rick Wright, disgruntled by the direction things were going with Depot Market Square, took on that endeavor and helped create another of the wonders of Bellingham.

The Fairhaven Village Green Committee was presented the Mayor's Arts Award that spring, but the greatest reward for any who were involved in the project is to see all that happens on the Green. Not a day goes by that some use is not made of it, from neighborhood workers lunching there, to kids playing tag, to concerts and Saturday night movies, to seasonal festivals. The Village Green has indeed become the heart of Fairhaven.

I was surprised and honored when I was told I would be presented the Liberty Bell Award by the Whatcom County Bar Association. For more than thirty years, the group had bestowed the award on non-attorneys who they felt had made a significant legal contribution to the community.

In presenting the plaque, attorney Dan Raas cited my work in defending the First Amendment and other civil liberties, working for civil rights on the Human Rights Task Force, and otherwise being involved in strengthening the community. With the PATRIOT Act casting a huge shadow on personal privacy, I shared, in accepting the honor, a favorite quote from Benjamin Franklin: "They that can give up essential liberty to obtain a little temporary safety deserve neither liberty nor safety."

Meanwhile, planning for the new Village Books building continued. After what seemed ages, we finally broke ground in February of 2004. While the building was being constructed, we were scrambling to plan layout, lighting, finishes, and fixtures, among a score of other details. And we were trying to add some interesting features.

We were inspired by "The Tree Project" at Whatcom Museum, for which Smith & Vallee Woodworks had created 55 pieces of furniture from a single bigleaf maple. We thought it would be great to have a piece of bookstore furniture made from the tree that would have to be removed from the front of the store property. It could be accompanied by a placard that would tell about the history of the tree—it had been a volunteer in a rubbish pile–and what had happened in Fairhaven during its life. I asked our friend Phil Ager if he could build us something interesting from the wood. He agreed.

When Matt Christman and I were talking about the new building one day, I mentioned the tree.

"Oh, you mean that black cottonwood?"

"Really, that's a black cottonwood? I thought it was an alder."

"No, it's definitely a black cottonwood."

I called Phil and said, "Phil, that tree's actually a black cottonwood. Is that wood good for anything besides burning?"

"Chuck," he said, "that wood isn't even good for burning."

That wasn't the end of art in the store. While looking over our building plans, we realized that there was a fairly sizable allowance for a light fixture in the rounded window at the Northeast corner of the store. Once again inspired, I called

Christopher Morrison's studio and talked with Julia Clifford, Christopher's assistant at the time, to see if he would be able to create something for the space using the amount we had in our lighting allowance. He said that he would come take a look at the space.

A couple of days later Julia called back. "We came and looked at the space," she said. "We didn't realize how big the area was. Christopher would still be happy to do something for the amount you mentioned, but to do real justice to the location, the piece should be much larger and would cost five times that amount."

After Julia suggested a couple of ways of raising money to pay for the glass sculpture, I told her I had an idea and would call her back. I called Dave Ebenal and asked if he and Bonnie would be willing to share the cost of the piece. He said he wanted to see a design and some of Christopher's glass first. Dee and I picked up a sketch of the proposed sculpture and some samples of blown glass and went to meet with Dave. He looked at the sketch and the glass and said, "Just have him make it elaborate."

"Helliconia Growing" was the first large public installation piece Christopher created, and in spite of costing five times what our lighting allowance had been, it was still priced at less than a fifth of what such a piece should have cost. The sculpture gets lots of attention from visitors and elicits many compliments. On one of his visits to the store, Dale Chihuly, one of Christopher's early mentors, signed books and chatted with Christopher under the piece.

We wanted something special for the outside of the building as well, and we decided to include tiles with the word for book in several of the languages of settlers of this area. You'll see *büch* in German, *livre* in French, *libro* in Spanish, etc. Because we wanted to include the Lummi language on one of the tiles, I called Bill James, a Lummi elder who has studied and taught the language to others.

"Bill, can you tell me what the Lummi word for book is?"

There was a long pause on the other end of the line. "The Lummi language was an oral, not written language, Chuck."

"Oh, right. Can you tell me the word for word?" Bill told me that *Skwai* means word in the Lummi language, and it now adorns one of the tiles that Joyce Russell made for us.

Construction went quickly, and we were able to move into the new space at the end of October, 2004. That move was something to behold.

Village Books closed at five o'clock on Saturday evening, October 23, in the space that it had occupied for more than 22 years, and reopened on Monday morning in its new location. In addition to the entire bookstore staff, we were helped by Phil Ager, who built the new fixtures; his wife Pam, a former children's book buyer at VB; Doug Ermini and David Spangler, who headed up our fixture-moving crews; and more than one hundred and fifty volunteers who showed up to help transport books and shelves from one building to the next. Many of the folks who helped still warmly recount that move, and we will be forever grateful to each of them.

Shortly after we opened the new space, our friend Jo Morgan, a gifted weaver, offered a beautiful tapestry to hang in the building. It was first shown in Jo's culminating show when she earned her Master of Fine Arts degree. It then hung in several shows, galleries, and in her own weaving studio. Still, she says she likes to think of Village Books as its "first home." When asked why she chose to hang it here, she said, "It's a fabulous space and one of my favorite businesses. For heaven's sake, why not?"

It was a challenge getting the piece displayed where it is, along the stairway to the mezzanine, but it does get a lot of attention there. To discourage folks from stroking the inviting texture of the tapestry, we hung another small woven piece next to it with a sign inviting folks to touch.

Another generous gift came from Brian and Marya Griffin.

When the Griffins bought an old house on 16th street, adjacent to their home, Brian found 11 bird's eye prints of Fairhaven in the attic. Such prints were used by developers in many cities to lure property buyers and, they hoped, the railroad terminus. The Fairhaven map was published in 1891 by the Fairhaven Land Company, and like many such maps, includes buildings that never existed, apparently to enhance the appearance of the place. One such building on the Fairhaven map is just to the east of the Fairhaven Hotel. The framed print hangs next to the elevator in the Parkside North area of the store and it's not uncommon to see someone trying to find his or her house on the map.

Between the turn of the century and the end of 2004, we hosted more than a thousand authors. Among them were dozens of the biggest names in publishing, including Pico Iyer, Richard Ford, Elizabeth Berg, Simon Winchester, Scott Turow, Sarah Dunant, Rick Bragg, David Guterson, Ursula Hegi, and David Guterson.

In addition, scores of local and regional authors visited the store. Some weeks, there were author events every night. Now when people called the store about events, they would often ask *who* was there that night rather than *if* someone would be here.

Two big off-site author events occurred nearly back to back during the holiday season of 2004. On the last day of November, beloved poet Gary Snyder packed the Bellingham High School auditorium and read his poetry to a most appreciative crowd. The ticketed event raised more than $4500 for North Cascades Institute.

Two nights later, in the same packed venue, David Suzuki talked about his book *Tree*. During the Q & A session, a woman asked, "Should we really be concerned about climate change?"

"You should be be scared shitless," replied Suzuki.

Ticket proceeds of more than $4000 were split between Whatcom Land Trust and Sustainable Connections.

The "Dear Reader" column of our 2004 holiday *Chuckanut Reader* said this: "As we come into our 25th Holiday season, we're as excited as we were as we approached our first in 1980." It's a good thing we were excited and energized, because the challenges of the latter half of the decade would soon be upon us.

Chapter 8

A Rollercoaster Ride
2005–2010

In March of 2005, Dee and I were invited to a dinner with author Cassandra King for her book *The Same Sweet Girls*. Cassandra is married to Pat Conroy, one of my all-time favorite writers.

I had first become aware of his work at the ABA convention in Atlanta in 1981. The paperback edition of *The Lords of Discipline* was just about to be released, and his publisher was handing out prepublication copies to booksellers. I picked one up, and devoured it on a post-convention vacation. I was hooked on Conroy.

As a convention breakfast speaker in 1986, for his novel *The Prince of Tides*, he created such buzz that booksellers read and recommended the book in numbers to make it a national bestseller. He returned as a speaker in 1995, prior to the publication of *Beach Music*, and I had the privilege of introducing Pat at a convention breakfast. Once again, he charmed and inspired the booksellers and, though not as critically acclaimed as *The Prince of Tides*, the book went on to top the bestseller charts.

During our dinner with Cassandra, she told us that she and Pat were recently featured in a magazine, and that a photographer had been engaged to do a shoot in their home. Before the photographer arrived, Pat had said, "I'm not going to do one of those shots with the two of us on the bed."

In spite of Pat's protests, the photographer had convinced him to do the shot that appeared in the magazine. She showed us a copy.

"I'd love to be able to tease him about that," I said.

"I'll give you his email address, please do," she said.

I sent the email telling him I couldn't believe he would allow himself to be in such a clichéd photograph. With his typical self-effacing Southern humor, Pat laughed off my ribbing and said that he was finally able to get Cassandra to admit she'd put me up to it.

Since we had spent years planning the new store, one might assume that we had carefully considered every detail, and that we had made no big mistakes. Wrong. In April, following the October move-in, we hosted our Independent Booksellers Consortium's spring idea exchange. This is a group of booksellers from twenty-five of the best stores in the country who have joined together to share practices and help each other with our businesses.

As part of each idea exchange, the host store is offered a critique session. One evening all of the attending booksellers tour the store with a list of criteria to evaluate. When the group meets the next day, the booksellers offer their ideas and suggestions for improvement.

What made this particular session special was the presence of Paco Underhill, author of *Why We Buy*, which has sold more copies than any other book about retail. The group gathered around the towering Underhill for some pre-tour tips. That's when I had my "Oh shit!" moment.

"Co...me over here," Paco said, elongating words to cope with his lifelong stutter, "I want to sho...w you something,"

With that he led the group to the top of the stairway leading down to the lower level of the store. I walked over and looked down as well.

"Wha...t do you see?" he asked.

I nearly fell down the stairs. The most apparent object was a copy machine, and there were hardly any books visible.

"I feel like I'm loo...king down into an office." Paco said. "Wh...y would I want to go down there?"

On Monday, after our colleagues had returned to their bookstores, I called our electrician and asked him to install an outlet in another location and move the machine. We placed a display table where the copy machine had been and added a large sign above the stairway, indicating that there were more books downstairs. It was an embarrassing way to learn of our mistake, but it would have been more embarrassing, and more costly, to have customers miss nearly half of the store.

In early August of 2005, while Dee, JoAnn and I were in San Francisco for the gift show, my cell phone rang. It was our friend Mitch Kaplan of Books & Books in Miami, who was president of ABA at the time.

"Chuck, I promised the Australian Booksellers Association that I would give a keynote for their convention," he said. "But there are so many things going on here that I just can't do it. Can you go in my place?"

"When?" I asked.

"The second week in September."

It was short notice and I had already committed to giving a presentation on basic bookstore finances at the PNBA fall show, but I said yes. I would just have to work out the details. Dee and I took the train to Portland for the PNBA show. The next morning I gave my presentation and headed for the airport.

The capital city of Canberra is an odd place. A compromise location, between Sydney and Melbourne, for the seat of Australian government, it was planned to be built halfway between the two cities on a sheep paddock—planned by an American, Walter Burley Griffin. Those who've read Bill Bryson's *In a Sunburned Country* will recognize Canberra as the place he called "an extremely large park with a city hidden in it." While watching a promotional video about the capital, he renamed it "Canberra - why wait for death."

Bryson also asserted that he couldn't find any place to eat near his hotel, except the hotel dining room itself. I found the same to be true. I arrived mid-day and wanted to walk somewhere for lunch, since I knew I'd be spending quite a bit of time in the hotel during the convention.

"Is there a pub nearby?" I asked at the front desk.

"Well, there's a place about a mile that way," she said, pointing south. "Or, you can walk across the Commonwealth Avenue Bridge into the city. That's about a mile north."

I chose the city center, visited a couple of small bookshops, had lunch, and wandered back to the hotel. During my stay I was able to visit the National Gallery of Australia and the National Museum of Australia, where an awards dinner was held. Another dinner was hosted in a boarding school dining hall that, to my mind, was just like Hogwarts.

I had arranged to fly through Sydney into the capital, spend four days, and fly straight back. Fortunately, wiser heads prevailed. When booksellers at the convention learned that I wouldn't see any other part of their vast country, they convinced me to cancel the Canberra to Sydney leg of my flight and ride back to Sydney with a couple who owned a store there. They booked me into a hotel on Sydney's harbor, just a short distance from the Opera House.

I was able to have dinner that night with Derek Dryden, owner of Better Read Than Dead, a bookstore in Sydney, and Sally Chilvers, the owner of a franchise bookstore in the city. The next morning Derek's wife, Maggie, gave me a quick tour of the city and several of its bookstores before I was whisked off to the airport for my flight home. Later, when friends heard about my journey, they joked that I'd spent as much time in the air as I had in Australia. It was a great trip, but never again will I go so far for such a short period of time.

Over the years I've come to believe that there are fewer than six degrees of separation. On one of Terry Brooks' visits to the store we began talking about where we grew up. I knew Terry was from Sterling, Illinois, and told him I was from Galva, another small Illinois town about sixty miles southwest of Sterling. I also mentioned that my Mom had a cousin in his hometown.

"You wouldn't, by chance, know an insurance agent named Tom Keeney, would you?" I asked.

"Tom Keeney? He's one of my Dad's best friends," Terry said. "He was at the country club when Dad and I had dinner there on my last visit."

When Roscoe Orman—Gordon from Sesame Street—was booked for an event, our friend Clyde Ford mentioned that he was a friend and asked to introduce him. And when "L.A. Law" stars Michael Tucker and Jill Eikenberry came to promote their book *Living in a Foreign Language*, we learned that our friends Michael Petryni and Cheryl Crooks had known them from their L.A. days.

On a recent trip to Argentina we were attending a wine tasting in Mendoza and talking with other attendees about where we were all from. When we mentioned Bellingham, a woman said, "You probably know my ex-husband. He's an author."

"What's his name?" I said.

"Steve Hodel," she said.

I told her that our friend Jill Bernstein had brought Steve to meet me and talk about a secretive book he was working on. It was about a police cover-up in Los Angeles, and he couldn't talk about details. I helped connect him with a couple of publishers. He published the book, *Black Dahlia Avenger*—though with a different publisher. In the book he asserts that his father, Dr. George Hodel, was the "Black Dahlia killer."

A few weeks after Village Books moved into its new space, Dee and I moved into our new space—a condominium above the store. We love being close to work. In fact, what would normally be a third bedroom is our office, wired with the store's computer and telephone systems.

We were often asked, prior to moving in, if we didn't feel like we'd be too close to work. "Will you ever be able to get away?" folks would ask. Truth be told, neither of us is a workaholic. Not that we don't work long hours, but we don't work when we don't want to work, and we like to be able to work when we want to.

When we lived away from the store, we were often frustrated by not having the one piece of paper we needed to complete a task at home. Though only three miles away, we knew by the time we got in and out of the store we would have burned up the better part of half an hour, and much more if we got caught in a conversation.

I've always been more of a night person. It's not unusual for me to settle into some task at my computer late in the evening, when phones aren't ringing and all is quiet. Do I work more hours now? I don't really know, but I know I'm more satisfied with the hours I do work.

Living in Fairhaven is a treat—literally. At last count there were nearly thirty restaurants, cafés, and other places to get food—all a few steps from our door. We do have to be careful, since being minutes away from good beer, great food, and gelato could prove unhealthy. Fortunately it's only three blocks to Bellingham Tennis Club and Fairhaven Fitness, and Dee does yoga less than two blocks away.

We also have a great back yard—the Fairhaven Village Green—and as I point out to friends, the parks department mows it for us. We are truly the target audience for an urban village, and no place tops Fairhaven for that distinction.

Since moving into our condo, we've hosted a number of

events. Some have been fundraisers, some have been author receptions, and some have been a combination of the two.

One of the first was with Mark Kurlansky, author of *Cod* and *Salt*. His new book was called *The Big Oyster*, and though it was a history of New York City, it did involve oysters. We partnered with the Drayton Harbor Community Oyster Farm and Purple Smile Wines to raise money for the oyster farm project. Forty guests plowed through forty dozen oysters and accompanying wines, and raised $1200 for the cause.

The author escort who brought Mark to the event was back a few nights later with another author, and said, "On the way to the car the other night, Mark Kurlansky said, 'I'll certainly come back here.'" I'm just afraid he'll expect oysters every time.

A little more than a year later we hosted another seafood event at our place. This time it was Trevor Corson with his book *The Zen of Fish*. Subtitled *The Story of Sushi from Samurai to Supermarket*, the book, which focused on a U.S. sushi school, had been getting lots of attention—NPR had featured Corson, and Jay McInerney had reviewed the book in *The New York Times*. His review included this:

Fortunately, the classroom scenes are intercut with authoritative, often amusing, chapters on sushi history, marine biology and the physiognomy of taste. While the students hack away at mackerel, Corson serves up bite-size explanations of the invention of soy sauce, the sex life of red algae and the importance of umami, that mysterious fifth taste that underlies so much of Eastern cuisine. His chapter on rice, a subject that Americans take for granted, is itself worth the price of the book.

At our event, "Chef Alex" Chavez prepared sushi, and Corson regaled the capacity crowd with facts and lore about sushi, including the tip that, in a good sushi bar, one should not add wasabi to the sushi because the sushi chef has included the correct amount.

As we moved through 2006, though we had become increasingly comfortable in our new bookstore space, and were loving living in Fairhaven, all was not sweetness and light in the book business. I wrote this short article called "What We Almost Lost" for the 2005 winter edition of the *Chuckanut Reader*:

On Wednesday morning, August 31, a shock wave surged through the world of book selling. Our friend and colleague, Clark Kepler, whose father founded Kepler's 50 years ago, had called together his staff and called it quits. "This is it," he said solemnly as he handed employees their last paychecks.

But fortunately, for us all, that was not "it." The town rallied, investors were found and Kepler's reopened on Saturday, October 8, with lines that a friend described as "like December 23rd."

And neither, unfortunately, is that "it." Independent bookstores and other independent businesses struggle daily with increased costs, lowered margins and the illusion that low prices are good for the economy, and that there's not a huge cost to be paid for them.

We often take for granted what we have. As Joni Mitchell put it, "Don't it always seem to go that you don't know what you got 'til it's gone?" When Kepler's customer Cristina Thorson talked to the *San Francisco Chronicle* the day of reopening, she said, "I was conscious before about my book-buying decisions, but I'm even more conscious now. I scold people now for buying online. When they get truculent I say, 'Look at what we almost lost.'"

As we enter another holiday shopping season, we hope you'll carefully consider all of your buying decisions—not just where you buy books. We hope you'll think about the special contributions local businesses make to the community and what it would be like without them. We hope you'll think about what we almost lost.

One could easily invoke a Shakespeare title here—"All's Well That Ends Well"—but the struggle hasn't ended. Kepler's is still in business, but when I talk with Clark, he reminds me what a short attention span people have.

In late spring of 2006, Neal Sofman, a longtime teaching colleague at bookseller schools, announced the closing of A Clean Well Lighted Place for Books in San Francisco. Following closely on the heels of that news came word that Cody's would close their original Telegraph Avenue store. Neal and his wife Anna opened a small neighborhood store, which continues to operate. Books Inc., another Bay Area indie, moved into Neal's old location, and Cody's kept their Fourth Street and San Francisco stores—for a while. Now, Cody's is gone.

Each time customers hear about an independent bookstore closing, we're asked the same questions: "How are you doing?" "Is Village Books okay?" "Are you going to survive?" The answers are not easy. This is a business of extremely low margins and rapidly increasing competition—in 1995 only 30% of books were being sold by non-bookstore retailers, and by 2007 that number had escalated to 55%.

Every store we know struggles to cut costs and increase sales in the face of a concentrated effort by competitors to eliminate us. Can you think of another reason major online companies would sell products for less than they pay for them?

The economy has created problems for many businesses all over the country, and Whatcom County has not been spared. 2009 retail sales, which were, like housing, overheated, dropped to a level not seen since 2005. Unfortunately, most costs did not drop.

Some think Dee and I are wealthy and that profitability doesn't matter. We even learned that a former employee thought we owned a house in Palm Springs. We don't. Let me put things in perspective: Dee and I used to be teachers, part of a shamefully underpaid group of dedicated people. We each have

Masters degrees. In the Bellingham School District—not known for its top-end salaries—with our degrees and years of experience, heading departments with as few as eight teachers, we would earn nearly twice what we are now paid.

Ah, but the profits! In the best years, bookstores, on average, took two percent of sales to the bottom line, and in recent years that number has slipped into the negative side of the ledger. So no one I know is doing this for the big bucks.

All of that said, we will continue to fight the good fight. We'll look for new business models. We'll cut costs where we can. We'll go on finding ways to add value. All we can ask of you is to think about what you really want. If you're happy with a world (or even your corner of the world) without a community bookstore, it doesn't matter where you buy your books. If you want to keep that bookstore—or any local business—it does matter. Lecture over.

In November of 2006, Phil Printz, relatively new to town, came to see me. We hadn't yet met, but a mutual friend sent him my way. He talked about community radio and the possibility of being involved in some programming with the station at the American Museum of Radio and Electricity. I shared a fantasy I had, inspired by friends at Square Books in Oxford, Mississippi, to have a radio variety show, centered around authors. I told him about *Thacker Mountain Radio*, their program featuring authors and music in an unrehearsed old-time radio format. He was intrigued.

We decided we'd give it a shot and thought we might launch the show the following spring. At the end of November, I learned that we had booked Erik Larson for an author's event at the store in January. A major theme of his new book, *Thunderstruck*, involved wireless inventor Guglielmo Marconi. Because of his role in the invention of radio and the fact that the museum had artifacts from Marconi's personal lab, it was too much to pass up. Though we were in the thick of the holiday season, with less than six weeks to put a show together, we decided to go forward.

We recruited The Walrus as our house band and invited the a cappella group The Honeybees and 14-year-old saxophonist Thomas Harris as musical guests. Jim Bertolino agreed to share his poetry in our Poets' Corner and Alan Rhodes, columnist for the Cascadia Weekly, wrote a special slice-of-life essay for the show. Floyd McKay had many years of experience as an interviewer on Portland's NBC affiliate station, and we asked him to interview Erik. Rich Donnelly, who had radio background, accepted our invitation to be the show's announcer. Phil became the producer and I the executive producer and program's host.

The afternoon of January 10 we were all extremely nervous, and not just about the show. A blizzard had moved in, and we feared our featured guest might not be able to make it up I-5. We also worried whether we'd have an audience if he did arrive. Late in the afternoon we talked with Erik, and he assured us he could plow his way to Bellingham. It also seemed likely the rest of the cast and crew would slip and slide their way to the studio.

At 6:30 that evening, when The Walrus began the warm-up music, there were more than forty intrepid souls in the audience. There were a few more by the time Rich, with theme music playing in the background, stepped to the microphone and began...

"Ladies & gentlemen, boys and girls, with music that will satisfy, poets and authors who will edify, coming to you from the studios of the American Museum of Radio and Electricity in beautiful downtown Bellingham, the city of subdued excitement, and brought to you by Village Books, it's time for the..."

At that point the Honeybees, in their '40s musical style, finished Rich's sentence by singing, "The Chuckanut Radio Hour," and our first show was underway. Some variation of that introduction has opened each of the thirty plus programs over the next three years. The theme music plays behind the announcer, and a recording of the Honeybees finishes each of the introductions.

Much of the format of the show remains the same as well. There is still a Poets' Corner, usually featuring a poet but occasionally with poetry readings by the cast. Alan Rhodes appears in one of the most beloved segments of each show, sharing one of his often-pointed and always-humorous essays, and we feature an author guest, usually interviewed by Floyd. Through that first year The Walrus was our house band, but though the members of that group have appeared in various configurations since, the house band concept has given way to a greater variety of musical guests. Beginning with the sixth show, Dee joined me as the program's co-host.

I wrote the script for the first show—something I learned was far more difficult than it might seem. I'd write and rewrite and finally get a segment I thought was pretty good, only to realize it took just a minute to perform, and the show was an hour long. Fortunately, Phil Printz's fiance (now wife) Leslie Clark stepped into the writing role and created most of the scripts over the next two and a half years. More recently Shelley Muzzy, Rich Donnelly, Leslie and I have formed a team that writes the show.

With the second show the Chuckanut Radio Players joined the cast to dramatize readings from the guest authors' books and on the fourth show their role expanded to a serial comedy— "The Bellingham Bean." "The Bean" is the ongoing story of three siblings—Michael, a frustrated artist, Bennie, who thinks he was born to be a comedian, and Polly, the queen of trivia— who run a coffee shop in downtown Bellingham. The adventures, or more accurately misadventures, of the Bean family have run the gamut from a runaway coffee cart to a collapsing mine shaft under their shop, and have explored a variety of the brothers' half-baked schemes to improve the business of the espresso bar.

The show with Susan Vreeland, author of *Luncheon of the*

Boating Party, the story of a Renoir painting, took on a distinctively French flavor. The serial comedy introduced a new character, the Beans' Auntie Sue Bean, who after a stint in a Parisian pastry school had taken the name Suzette Legume. Suzette is played by Dee, who joined the regular cast of Robert Muzzy as Michael, Leon Charbonneau as Bennie, and Shelley Muzzy, who plays Polly.

"The Bean" has welcomed several guest players as well. Shortly after Sam Green was named Washington State's Poet Laureate, we invited him to be our poet on the show. "I love old radio," he said. "I have tapes of old radio shows that I play in my car. Do I get to be part of a radio skit?" Sam did, indeed, get written into "The Bean," and proved that his talents stretch far beyond poetry. Other authors who have taken guest roles in the segments have included Stephanie Kallos, one of Michael's love interests whose character was more interested in taking over the espresso bar than she was in him; Garth Stein, who played a hamster; and Garrison Keillor, who played himself.

Though most of the shows that first year were held at the American Museum of Radio and Electricity, we recorded three of them in other venues. We had been bringing Sherman Alexie to town for several years and knew that our regular spot wouldn't accommodate the crowd he would draw, so we booked the auditorium at Bellingham High. We packed more than seven hundred people in that evening for a spectacular show.

A group of people had put together a low-power radio station at Van Zandt and invited us to record the show in their community hall. They had warned us that each evening a train passed through at the very same time and very close to the building in which the show would be recorded. Leslie went to great lengths to create dialogue that could be slipped into the script when the train created its havoc. Throughout the show the players anxiously awaited the approach of the locomotive. It never came.

In celebration of Banned Books Week we invited the president of the American Booksellers Foundation for Free Expression (ABFFE), Chris Finan, to be our guest at a special dinner theater presentation of the show in Northwood Hall. Chris had recently penned the book *From the Palmer Raids to the Patriot Act*. It was, as the subtitle indicated, "A History of the Fight for Free Speech in America."

Jack Keith, former editor of *The Bellingham Herald* and a journalism professor at WWU, in Floyd's absence, interviewed Chris. Dee read from a recent anthology of poems by prisoners at Guantanamo. Chris had this to say on his blog after his visit:

It was amazing to see the profusion of talent that Chuck and Dee have tapped. There were writers, actors and musicians, and the one who impressed me the most was Dee, who took one of the leading roles in the radio drama. I didn't know that she had studied theater in college, but there could be no doubt about it after hearing her read so movingly from *Poems from Guantanamo*.

Having outgrown our space at the museum, we moved the show to the Crystal Ballroom of the Leopold Residence Center, and they became co-sponsors of the show. At times we miss the atmosphere of the museum studio, but the extra space has allowed us to welcome larger audiences, and some of the residents of the Leopold are able to regularly attend the performances. Still, there are times we record the show at other locations.

In June of our first year, we were asked to provide the entertainment on the Fairhaven Village Green before one of the Saturday evening outdoor cinema presentations. We gladly accepted. Our guest that evening was Kate Trueblood, and The Senate was slated as the musical entertainment. Threatening clouds became pouring rain, the evening's film was cancelled, and we quickly scrambled to move the show into the Village Books Readings Gallery, a few feet away. Because the ominous weather had kept many folks away, we were able to cram in everyone who did show up. Fortunately our musical guests, stuffed into the back corner, were just three players and not a full jazz band or choir.

The next summer we were invited back to provide pre-film entertainment, this time with returning Radio Hour guest Sherman Alexie and his film *The Business of Fancy Dancing*. We knew we wouldn't be able to move inside, so Doug Borneman, the film series producer, had provided a large tent on the stage. We had vowed that the show would go on, rain or shine. Fortunately the tent wasn't needed, the Village Green was packed, and the show went off without a hitch.

In May of 2009, we welcomed Tom Robbins to the stage of Boundary Bay's beer garden, and like that first occasion on the Village Green, rain threatened all day. Late in the afternoon the clouds parted and the sun shone through, and just as my weather anxieties were easing my phone rang. It was Tom.

"Chuck, I have some really bad news," he said. "Alexa was attacked by a raccoon last night. I took her to the hospital and was up most of the night." He went on to explain that their small dog had been dragged under the back step by the raccoon and his wife had tried to rescue it, only to be attacked. I imagined this was just the prelude to his telling me he would have to cancel, but Tom continued, "I'll be there, but Alexa won't be with me. I'm pretty beat, so we may have to shorten up the signing at the end."

Tom did arrive, the program went well, and no book went unsigned.

Music has always been a central and popular part of the show. We had known Chuck Dingee, Joe Young, Walt Burkett, Jaimie Shea and Michael O'Neal of The Walrus for years before asking them to join us on our first show. They became our house band, playing a warm-up set before we began recording, and some numbers during the show. In addition we invited musical guests for each show. The Senate joined us on the second program. We had first encountered Nick, Oliver, and Andrew at a North Cascades Institute birthday celebration. I bought their CD and immediately became a groupie, arranging for them to play at the Fairhaven farmers' market, showing up at nearly every one of their Bellingham gigs, and inviting them to play on the Radio Hour. The group had such a popular reception that they appeared more times than any other musical guests.

We've hosted an eclectic mix of musicians over the years, playing everything from rock and roll to folk to country to jazz. Besides The Senate, a few other folks have played more than once on the show. Ron Hardesty first brought his own brand of country western music to the show in November of our first year. Following Ron's first number, Rich asked if it would be possible for him to play a request and, after being told that we needed to speed things along, suggested that we were "squeezing all the joy out of life." He said he just wanted to request a song to celebrate a special occasion.

"Well, I wouldn't call listening to "The Chuckanut Radio Hour," 'squeezing all the joy out of life,' but I take your point," I said. "What's the occasion?"

"It's someone's sixtieth birthday," Rich said. "Someone here on the stage I might add."

I admitted it was, indeed, my sixtieth, and received a round of applause.

"So back to my request," Rich said. "Ron, could you sing a birthday song for Chuck?"

Without hesitation Ron began singing, "Old man river, that old man river..." After some uproarious laughter, the crowd was coaxed into singing "Happy Birthday" with Ron.

Ron returned recently for a western-themed show that featured authors Mark Spragg and Laura Bell. He does western music pretty well for a lawyer from Michigan.

In addition to being heard via recording in the opening

of each show, the Honeybees returned for our first anniversary show, opening the show with a live rendition of the jingle and providing us with more of their harmonious tunes. Millie and the Mentshn has twice brought their popular klezmer music our way and another group has joined us twice as well... under two different names. Stone Soup first played with us at the Crystal Ballroom, and then provided the music for our third pre-movie appearance on the Fairhaven Village Green under their new name, Brother Dalton's Euphonic Elixir.

There have been a few "family" connections among our musical guests. Rich's son Peter was part of the Bellingham High Show Stoppers, when they performed during a program with Sherman Alexie at BHS. Marinus Van de Kamp brought his jazz group, The Marinus Trio, to the show. His wife Irene was part of our "Cinco de Mayo Seven." And, Jeff Mack, himself a former VB staffer, played piano, including his own compositions.

Other musical guests have included Reid Kerr, King Ludd, Shaken Not Stirred, and Mocking Bird. We've only had one show without live music, and that was my mistake. When planning the French-themed show featuring Susan Vreeland, I had sought out a French Cabaret band. I found a group in Seattle—with one Bellingham band member—and booked them for the show. As time drew near for them to set up, they still hadn't arrived. When I called the local member, I learned I'd given the group a different date. Though we didn't have music for the show that night, Tim Kraft, our sound engineer, was able to splice in some French tunes before the show aired.

The most unusual Radio Hour was one in which we showed a film. "On radio?" you might ask. On radio. Dave Weich had begun creating a short author film series at Powells for screening by independent bookstores around the country. His documentary with Ian McEwan, author of *On Chesil Beach*, was the first of three that he produced. The others were about David Halberstam's *The Coldest Winter* and an anthology by fifty writers called *State by State*.

Because we record the show with a live audience, we decided that we would show the twenty-minute film, then edit the sound track before putting the show on the air. The week before the live program, Phil, Leslie, Dee, and I sat down to watch the film and make decisions about where we would have to chop out pieces to make it work for radio. The second time we played the film we turned off the picture and just listened to the sound track. As it turned out, we didn't have to cut anything from the film. When the visuals were taken away, it played like a radio script.

I hadn't given much thought to the content of the film before I booked the musical guests for that night. We had heard the Bellingham Youth Jazz Band and knew they would be a great addition to the show. What I had forgotten was that *On Chesil Beach* was about a wedding night... the part after the wedding ceremony. As the film played and I watched the faces of the adolescent boys in the group, I began to imagine the complaints I might receive from some of the accompanying parents. On the contrary, we were told that some of the kids were currently enrolled in a sex education class and that the evening had fit right into their studies. Sometimes you just get lucky.

It takes some chutzpah to invite Garrison Keillor to be a guest on a radio variety show, particularly one inspired by his program. We were thrilled when he agreed, and took great care to send him the rundown and script for the show to be certain that he was comfortable doing everything we were asking.

The plan had been for an author escort to drive him from Seattle that day, but at the last minute he changed his plans and flew to Bellingham. I met him at the airport and drove him to Fairhaven Village Inn. The conversation in the car was relaxed and friendly. He was interested in knowing what mountain he was looking at—Mount Baker—and how our bookstore was doing. As he's also a bookstore owner, we concluded that we were both getting by.

"And what would you like me to do tonight?" he asked.

I nearly choked, but replied as calmly as I could, "Did you see the script I sent?"

"Oh no, but that's okay," he said.

We had sold out the Performing Arts Center at Western Washington University—a thousand and forty seats—and we certainly didn't want any big glitches. During the pre-show run-through it became obvious that it would be okay. At one point where there was a choice of how something might be done, our producer Leslie Clark turned to Garrison and asked, "Which way would you rather do this?"

"Just tell me what to do," he said. In the break between the run-through and the show Garrison graciously videotaped a promo spot for the Pickford Film Center in support of their capital campaign. Tickets for the show had raised more than $10,000 for the Pickford.

In the opening moments Rich said, "Who would ever have thought we'd have our hero and role model on our show?"

I said, "You know, that reminds me, Rich. Remember our first show in January of '07, when I said that people were comparing 'The Chuckanut Radio Hour' to 'A Prairie Home Companion,' and you scoffed and said I was no Garrison Keillor. And said with no tact at all, I might add, that I should keep my day job."

Rich became apologetic, but moments later while asking Garrison about his recently-opened bookstore, *Common Good Books*, Rich told him, "Chuck said he hoped you were half as good at the book business as you were as a radio host, and I said he should hope to be a fraction as good a radio host as..." At that point I interrupted saying, "Okay, Rich, let's not go back there..." And we moved on into the show with Keillor making jokes about Bellingham's motto, "The City of Subdued Excitement."

We had written him into nearly every segment of the show,

and he was a trooper. He threw himself into the show, picking up on local elements and ad libbing. During the episode of "The Bellingham Bean," Garrison played himself. He was asked in the episode to play "Stump the Barista," a trivia game, with the character Polly. The theme was old time radio. The questions were scripted but, once again, Garrison ad libbed and began asking questions for which Shelley Muzzy, who plays Polly, didn't know the answers. Shelly, also a trooper, acted her way through the segment, which had become even funnier with Keillor's additions.

Musical guests on the show were Courtney Fortune and The Senate. Courtney, a student at U.S.C., was regularly in our bookstore as a young reader, and was a winner of both our bookmark contest and kids' writing contest—a multitalented young woman. Even when she was in high school, she performed jazz vocals in professional venues. She was thrilled when we invited her to join us, and we were even more thrilled when she accepted. She and Garrison sang "Ain't Misbehavin."

This was the sixth time The Senate played for "The Chuckanut Radio Hour." They seem to wow everyone who hears them, Garrison Keillor included. He lauded them for playing "brilliant Dionysian music that you can't play past the age of thirty." He also said, "I've never heard of a rock and roll band named for a deliberative body before. And they're a great, great, wonderful group." After the show Keillor asked about their CD and insisted on paying for it when they attempted to give him one. He also asked about "Molly," a song they played that wasn't on the album. He gave them his email address and asked if they could email an MP3.

Alan Rhodes has been a regular part of the show since the very first night. We knew his essays from the *Cascadia Weekly*, but soon learned that his delivery style was half the fun. When Dee introduced him during this show, Alan began:

"Whoa, I have never worked a gig this big. How did everybody hear about me?

(uproarious laughter)

"Okay, seriously for just a moment, it's an amazing honor and privilege to be on the program with my hero and role model, Garrison Keillor. But I would like to comment on something that's been bothering me for a while. I'm disturbed that from the very beginning 'The Chuckanut Radio Hour' has been unfairly compared to 'A Prairie Home Companion.' We've been called a 'Prairie Home Companion' knock-off and a 'Prairie Home Companion' wannabe, and our show is not in any way like 'A Prairie Home Companion.' We are a stand-alone, one-of-a-kind, original radio show, and I just wish all those comparisons would stop. Okay, thanks for letting me get that off my chest, and now I can do my piece. Okay, here goes.

"Well, it's been a quiet week in Bellingham, my hometown."

Once again, the auditorium shook with laughter.

Alan has been one of the biggest surprises on the show. Each month, without fail, he entertains us with his humorous insights on everything from the names of roads in the county to local political issues. His piece has become one of my favorite parts of the show.

Alan's piece that night featured some of Keillor's Lake Wobegon characters in a visit to Bellingham. Keillor responded this way in his own monologue:

"It's wonderful to be part of this show and then come and be surprised by an account by Alan of a visit to Bellingham by people from Lake Wobegon. I thought I knew everything going on in Lake Wobegon, but evidently people are sneaking out of town without my being aware of it and coming out here. And to miss them by just a few days is a disappointment to me."

After the show Garrison began signing books in the lobby. In a short time, because it was hot and crowded inside, he led the crowd out onto the plaza and continued to sign books for an hour and a half under a full moon on that warm September night.

Linda Roberts Sundeleaf worked in banking for years and was managing the main branch of Key Bank when she discovered the early retirement option she had been offering to other employees was also available to her. She approached us saying, "I've always wanted to work at Village Books." We hired her immediately.

Two years after coming to the store and helping to set the customer service bar even higher than it had been, Linda was diagnosed with breast cancer. I can only hope if I ever face such an extreme challenge, I can do it with the class and grace that she constantly mustered. Five years later our staff offered this tribute to her in *The Chuckanut Reader*:

During the night of April 28 we lost our dear friend and colleague Linda Sundaleaf as her graceful and courageous dance with cancer ended after five years. In the seven years she worked here she was a constant source of enthusiasm and inspiration for all of us. Whether running the Village Books book club, organizing magazines, or just working with customers, she was a constant ray of sunshine. That's a cliché, we know, but it fit her. She was passionate about her dogs, gardening, playing games, her husband Charlie, Johnny Depp (as a pirate!), and of course, books! She will be deeply missed by all of us...

Though many of our travels might be hyperbolically referred to as "out of this world," one experience was almost literally that. I received a message on my voice mail that reminded me of Ed McMahon's Publishers Clearing House pitches. I, according to the call, had won a weightless flight. Just as I reached for the delete button, I recognized the name of the publisher, Quirk Books. They had conducted a contest to promote one of their books, *The Space Tourist's Handbook.* I had forgotten that I had entered, but, to my astonishment, my name had been drawn.

When I returned the call I learned that Quirk would take me to the Kennedy Space Center at Cape Canaveral, where I would board a specially modified 727 owned by Zero G, and experience weightlessness, just like astronauts-in-training and in the same way the weightless scenes were filmed for *Apollo 13.* By visiting Zero G's website I also learned that if I had wanted to do this on my own, it would have cost several thousand dollars.

Our national convention in 2007 was in New York, so when it was over, Dee and I drove to Florida, taking time to visit bookstores and friends along the way. On Friday, June 8th, I arrived at the Zero G flight center, donned my flight suit, ate the light breakfast they provided, and downed the anti-motion-sickness prescription they advised that everyone take.

Thirty of us, ranging in age from a teenager to a couple of septuagenarians, were soon airborne. The pilot took us west, over the Gulf of Mexico, looking for enough airspace to maneuver. Once he found room, he began flying the repeating porpoise-like pattern of a steep climb followed by a deep dive. With each of the parabolas, we floated in midair, turning somersaults, doing handstands, tossing NERF balls, and trying to catch in our mouths M&M's as they floated in space, or globs of water as they glugged from our water bottles.

No one got sick and everyone had a great time. On the bus, returning to the flight center, I struck up a conversation with the woman sitting across the aisle. She had absolutely loved the experience, as the video we received later would clearly show. We chatted most of the way back to the post-flight reception. There she was introduced to the entire group. "Ladies and gentlemen," said the host,"we have a special guest with us today. Please welcome Stephen Hawking's daughter, Lucy."

Music stores and ticket outlets had done midnight releases for some time, but until the fourth of J.K. Rowling's books, *Harry Potter and the Goblet of Fire*, was published, we'd never heard of a midnight release party for a book. That didn't stop us, or hundreds of other bookstores.

When book three, *Harry Potter and the Prisoner of Azkaban*, was released the previous year, we had thrown an evening party on the day of its release. But with book four we kept the store open from midnight, when the book went on sale, until 2am. At 3pm the following afternoon, we had a party with costumes, contests, magic, and Hogwarts treats.

With the publication of *Harry Potter and the Order of the Phoenix*, we once again held a midnight release party. The publication date fell on our anniversary weekend, so the activity was amazing. As before, there were games and treats, and magic by Scott Ochletree.

With the sixth and seventh books in the series, we began donating a portion of the proceeds to Whatcom Literacy Council. For *Harry Potter and the Half Blood Prince*, we gave $5 from the purchase of each book, totaling $3,150. Two years later we upped the ante and, because the book was released on 7/21, we gave $7.21 from the sale of each copy of *Harry Potter and the Deathly Hallows* to WLC, for a total of $8,724.10.

The popularity of the series had grown so strong that parties for both the sixth and seventh books were held on the Fairhaven Village Green. Many came costumed—both kids and adults—and Harry Potter could be spotted everywhere. After the sixth book party, bookseller Dennis Scott admitted to still being "buzzed" by the activity the next morning. "The looks on kids' faces were great, and they were all so thankful for the party and the book. It was amazing," he said.

In November of 2008, Deb Slater asked Dee and me to appear on her KVOS Television program, "Experience Northwest." We talked about holiday books, and after taping the segment, Deb asked if we would like to be part of the show each week. "Footnotes with Village Books" was born.

Dee, Sarah Hutton, or I appear in most of the segments. Often Dee and I together talk with Deb about books from a particular genre, recent prize-winning books, or perhaps books suitable for book groups. Sarah generally focuses on children's and young adult books, and occasionally Nan Macy, Cindi Williamson, Lindsey McGuirk, or another staff member will record a special segment for the show. The program is aired three times each week. Air times and many of the archived programs can be found at www.VillageBooks.com.

When Jim hit the twenty-year mark in 2008, we queried one of his friends for ideas of places to send him. She offered several possibilities, but it seemed he had long wanted to explore the Cotswolds. We found a walking tour company and packed him off to England, where he spent a week walking from village to village, staying in B&B's along the way. He finished up the trip with a little time in London and charmed all of us on his return with a terrific slide show of his adventure.

As far back as 1991, when the Bellingham Public Library celebrated its Centennial, Village Books participated in community-wide book programs. That year we helped organize a "Centennial Book Faire" that included nearly thirty Northwest authors and featured keynoter Ivan Doig.

Ten years later, inspired by Nancy Pearl's idea for a one

city, one book program, we joined with the local libraries and brought in Terry Kay, author of To *Dance With the White Dog* and numerous other books, for a "Catch 'em Reading" program. It was an ambitious undertaking, with a kick-off event with the author in March, and two weeks of events in October, with Terry in attendance.

It apparently took us seven years to recover, because it wasn't until 2008 that the group launched "Whatcom Reads," a one community, one book program. Sherman Alexie's book *The Absolutely True Diary of a Part-time Indian* was the first book chosen, and Sherman came to town for a three-day whirlwind of activities in February of 2009.

For 2009/2010 we partnered with "The Big Read," an initiative of the National Endowment for the Arts in partnership with the Institute of Museum and Library Services and Arts Midwest, who provided funding and materials for the program. Tobias Wolfe, author of *Old School*, was the chosen author. He came to Bellingham in February of 2010 for community presentations.

Border Songs by Jim Lynch has been chosen as the 2010/2011 book, with his book *The Highest Tide* chosen for young adults. Jim will spend three days in the community in early 2011, discussing his novel set near Blaine, along the U.S./Canada border.

The "Whatcom Reads" program has created lots of attention throughout the county by encouraging folks to read and discuss the same book. One can find more information about the project at www.whatcomreads.org.

Our most recent trip to London came about in an unusual manner. We were at our national convention in New York and stopped to chat with our friend Oren Teicher of the ABA office.

"I was just talking with folks from the London Book Fair,"

he said. "They're interested in getting more U.S. booksellers to the fair, and wanted ABA to help arrange that. I suggested they should talk with you two. You might want to stop by their booth and talk with Emma House."

We presumably came to Oren's mind because of our love of travel and the number of booksellers we know. We had a short talk with Emma that day and agreed to keep in touch. As our conversations and correspondence continued over the next few months, we agreed to recruit a group of booksellers to go to London for the fair in April of 2008.

Through notes to friends in the business and announcements in trade publications, we gathered a group of twenty-three. The staff at the London Book Fair had arranged a convenient hotel at very good rates, offered us free admission to the fair, and planned many special events for us. The cost for the attending booksellers was a fraction of what it would otherwise have been, and Dee and I, as the organizers, had our way paid.

While Book Expo America (BEA) is very much aimed at booksellers, the London Book Fair is not. In fact, we were a bit surprised that they had gone to such lengths to bring us over when we learned that some London booksellers don't even bother to take the tube to the event. While BEA is crawling with authors, few were in attendance in London. This fair was much more about selling foreign rights than promoting books to bookstores.

None of us found very good business reasons to be there, but we did have a great time. Two dinners with British booksellers had been arranged—one hosted by the Fair and the other by Simon & Schuster. Carolyn Reidy, the CEO of Simon & Schuster, was seated to my right at the dinner, and I asked her what exactly she did at the fair.

"I don't go to the fair," she said.

"Really? Then what are you doing here in London?"

"I'm here to have dinner with you," she said.

"You're joking."

"No," she said. "In the morning I'm going to Paris with my husband, and I'll come back after the fair is over to get some real work done."

We were also treated to a lunch with Sebastian Faulks, a tour of the Globe Theatre, and a literary pub crawl of Bloomsbury. None of us were sorry we went.

Over the years, Village Books has been given numerous awards—Dee was Business Woman of the Year in 1986; the store was a two-time finalist for Business of the Year; we've twice been awarded the Mayor's Arts Award; Rotary deemed me a Paul Harris Fellow (and told us the award extended to Dee as well); The Washington Education Association honored us with their Community Service Award; Governor Gardner gave us a volunteerism award, and Governor Gregoire presented the store with a Commute Smart Employer Champion award; I was given the Pacific Northwest Writers Association's Open Book award; *Bellingham Business Journal*'s readers named VB the Most Community-Minded Business; and readers of the *Herald* and the *Weekly* have regularly named us Bellingham's best bookstore.

We've been honored and humbled by every recognition. But the one that shocked us was the 2008 Washington State Outstanding Philanthropic Small Business Award. In granting the award, the Association of Fundraising Professionals said, "Village Books is a community leader through philanthropy, education, and activism. The Bellingham bookstore is part of the fabric of the community, connecting individuals and causes through the store's newsletter, book signings, and fundraising events in support of community good works."

Standing before an audience of more than twelve hundred people at the National Philanthropy Day awards ceremony in Seattle, watching a professionally-produced video about our community involvement, sent shivers down our spines. And it reinforced for us exactly what this has all been about—building community, one book at a time.

Chapter 9

The Future
2010–??

I seriously thought about leaving the pages of this chapter blank, and while it might be seen as a lame joke, it would also have some merit. After all, while I am concerned about the future of literacy and books, it won't be booksellers who decide that future. It will be you and other readers.

That said, let me frame the question about the future of Village Books, and perhaps all bookstores, in today's context. Where are we in 2010, and where might we be going? Where we are today might be best understood in reviewing the big changes we've seen in the past thirty years.

One of the biggest changes has come in the organization of publishing itself, as the industry has taken two seemingly contradictory directions. First, there's been massive consolidation. Bantam, Fawcett, Ballantine, Doubleday, and others were separate publishers. Now they're combined under Random House, which is owned by the German company Bertlesman, the largest publisher in the world.

Other publishers have similarly consolidated, and with the consolidation has come a different philosophy of management. Publishing companies used to be controlled primarily by editors. Now accountants have much more say. This consolidation, when linked with the discounting retailers have used to gain market share, has driven the treatment of books as commodities.

The flip side is that technology has put publishing into the hands of many—increasing numbers of authors are self-publishing, and more publishing companies have been created. So we have huge conglomerates that dominate mainstream publishing, and thousands of small publishers constantly springing up.

In that same time publishers, eager to get their books to the widest markets, have come to rely less on bricks and mortar bookstores and more on selling their books through a wide variety of outlets. Virtually every type of retail store now sells some books.

The retail bookstore scene has also changed radically. Since the early 90s, just among Borders, Barnes and Noble, and Books-A-Million, more than 1400 large bookstores have been created. Facing that competition, a large number of independent bookstores have closed. When I became president of ABA in 1992, the association had nearly 4500 members; today there are about a third of that. The indie market share likewise shrank from about 17% of all books sold to around 9%. I often joke about those figures as what my presidency did for ABA and indie bookstores.

In the mid-90s, online selling of books began to chisel away at another piece of the bookstore business. While bookstores had long sold books by mail order (online selling *is* mail order), the new mode of ordering via computer instead of by phone, coupled with heavy discounting, boosted this channel of book sales.

None of this might be bad news for bookstores if more books were being purchased. In fact, sales of books have not grown in proportion to population growth. So we have a limited number of books being sold by an increasing number of sellers. Bookstores are suffering "death by a thousand cuts."

At the same time, margins—among the lowest in all of retail—have not increased much, while costs have skyrocketed, particularly occupancy costs. Many of the bookstores that have closed over the past few years were shuttered, at least in part, because of escalating rents.

Throw into the mix electronic books, and this makes the "perfect storm" of the early '90s look like a minor squall. With the advent of the Sony Reader, Kindle, iPad, and other readers, an increasing number of books are being read on a device, rather than in printed form. While this number is not yet large, it is one more sliver of a constantly shrinking piece of the pie.

Village Books offers ebooks. We sell them on our website, and we sell cards in the store that allow one to download the book from a device connected to the internet. While we'll continue to improve the offerings and the technology for acquiring this form of books, it's difficult to compete with the big players in this arena.

There is also a lot of uncertainty about what portion of books will ultimately be read as ebooks. In considering that question, I'm reminded of a meeting I attended about fifteen years ago. An industry council had been formed by ABA, consisting primarily of the CEOs of the largest publishing companies. As a past-president of the ABA, I was one of a handful of booksellers in the group. At that meeting, the topic was ebooks—yes, fifteen years ago.

We were joined by two consultants from McKinsey & Company, likely the best known and most highly respected management consulting firm in the world—they consult with more than 70% of *Fortune* magazine's list of most admired companies. We spent the afternoon discussing the future of ebooks. The McKinsey folks facilitated and brought their expertise and experience to the table.

Each of the CEOs in the room admitted that he or she had little sense that ebooks would be a big part of their publishing future. No one really seemed to know how to move forward with the new format in their business plans.

At the end of the afternoon the McKinsey consultants summarized the discussion, bringing their own research and experience to bear. One of the consultants said, "Electronic books are likely to be a part of the publishing future, but not likely a huge part. We would recommend you pay attention to them, but not commit a lot of resources."

"Just to put this into perspective, however," said the other consultant, "you should also know that we were the folks who told the phone companies that cell phones weren't going anywhere."

I'm not sure the picture is much clearer today. It is certain that ebooks have arrived. It's still highly uncertain what portion of the market they will grow to be, or exactly how stores like ours will participate in selling this form of publication.

When Village Books first opened, we billed ourselves as "The Bookshop for Browsing." We knew that people valued leisurely browsing of books, taking the time to make up their minds about which they might want to spend more time reading. Bookstores have, in fact, been showrooms for books. If, however, someone uses the bookstore as the showroom, and then purchases elsewhere, the store has costs and no revenue.

This is partly true for author events as well, since most events are free. We bring authors in to interact with readers for a variety of reasons, including encouraging the purchase of the book. There are, of course, costs associated with bringing authors to the store. As with browsing, if folks come to events but book sales are not commensurate with costs, we have a problem.

It's clear that people like browsing and author events, and we love providing these experiences for our customers. What is less clear is how the bookstore can "monetize" the value of those services. If books continue to be viewed as commodities and purchased at the lowest price, how will bookstores, including Village Books, be compensated?

So that's where we find ourselves in 2010—relatively stagnant sales of books, with an increasing number of competitors selling them; books being considered a commodity; increasing costs of operation; the advent of ebooks, with some limits on how we can "play" in that arena; and difficulty "monetizing" our current business model. Is it time for independent booksellers, including Village Books, to fall on our swords?

I don't think so. Though the challenges seem daunting, I believe that we still add value in the world of books, whether in print or electronic. I also believe we add value to the community as a literary and intellectual center and as a supporter of many of the organizations and causes that make this a richer place to live.

I am equally clear that what got us here won't take us forward. New business models will be required, and we continue to explore those. One major initiative, begun late in 2009, is our investment in print-on-demand technology.

For more than ten years we've been following the development of equipment for printing and binding books in the store. Three factors led to our recently taking the plunge: 1) Millions of books are now available to print in-store, and that number grows daily. These include out-of-print books in the public domain as well as in-print books from more and more publishers. 2) Many more authors want to self-publish, whether for personal family distribution or to sell their books. 3) Village Books wants to publish some books, including books of local interest that were once in-print, and those that might not otherwise be published.

"You're really on the cutting edge," said one reporter about our Espresso Book Machine.

"I think that's called the bleeding edge," I replied.

We have no expectations that this venture will meet with instant success or bring in an exceptional amount of revenue. However, you hold in your hands the fifth book published by our imprint, Chuckanut Editions; we've printed a handful of books on-demand for folks; and we've worked with nearly two dozen authors in self-publishing their books.

All of this has happened in less than nine months. We have more books in the works that we will publish; access to on-demand titles—including both in-print and public domain books—increases on an almost daily basis; and individuals regularly contact us about self-publishing their books.

Is this the future of bookselling? We think it is part of the future. When we installed the Espresso Book Machine in the fall of 2009, we were the first store on the West Coast to have one of the machines. Now there are three others within one hundred miles. At least there are a few of us in the Northwest who think there is some future in this. Or perhaps there's something in the water.

As suggested, ebooks offer a different kind of challenge for independent bookstores. Currently there are a number of devices on which ebooks may be read, and all ebooks are not compatible with all devices. Kindle, perhaps the best known device, is proprietary to Amazon, so ebooks we sell cannot currently be loaded onto that device.

A big change is expected soon, as Google launches ebooks that will be "device agnostic," meaning they may be read on nearly any device. Google will work with all ebook outlets, including independent bookstores like Village Books.

Though it is not at all certain what portion of the market will move to ebooks, where the pricing of the format will settle, or exactly how folks will buy and download them, it does seem likely that we will not be cut totally out of the market. We hope to be able to provide folks their books in whatever format they choose to purchase them.

What about retirement? Dee and I have slightly different perspectives on that question. While both of us would like some more time away, she's more inclined to totally give up the day-to-day work and step away from the business. I must admit that I don't fully understand the concept of retirement. I like much of what I do, and am in no hurry to give it up.

The reality of being in our sixties with no clear succession plan does give us pause. So, as we explore the future of the independent bookstore business, we're also exploring the specific future of Village Books.

That future will depend heavily on what transpires over the next few years in the wider world of publishing and bookselling, and specifically at Village Books. It will depend on where you buy your books—or ebooks, or... And it will depend on our finding an ongoing, workable business model for Village Books.

Though the challenges may seem daunting, they are also exciting. Solving problems can be fun. Years ago I told folks that I would quit doing this when it quit being fun. It's still fun.

When we're asked if we have regrets, I can't help thinking of the Frank Sinatra line, "too few to mention." We've been extremely fortunate. For thirty years we've led a life that we once couldn't have imagined. We've had great coworkers, made great friends, traveled in fascinating places, and met amazing people. And, along the way, we've been part of building a great community, one book at a time.

Early in our bookselling career I was fortunate to meet David Schwartz of the Harry W. Schwartz Bookshops in Milwaukee. Regrettably, both the bookshops and David are now gone. Many of us looked to him as the conscience of bookselling, and his words nicely sum up how Dee and I feel about bookselling:

"Bookselling was and is for me a cultural and political expression, an expression of progressive change, of challenge to oppressive authority, of a search for a community of values which can act as an underpinning of a better world. The true profit in bookselling is the social profit; the bottom line, the measure of the impact of the bookshop on the community."

Amen, David.

Colophon

The text for this book was set in Times New Roman, a typeface designed by Stanley Morison and Victor Lardent in 1931 for the British newspaper, *The Times*. It is based on an older font named Plantin, but redesigned for legibility and economy of space. The typeface was used by the newspaper for forty years. *The Times* has switched fonts five times since 1972, but all have been based on the original New Roman font.

This book was designed and composed by Rod Burton of Roderick C. Burton - Art & Design

Printed and bound on the Espresso Book Machine at Village Books, Bellingham, Washington